Teach Smarter, Not Harder

Building a Sound Foundation
for a Successful Career

by
Sharon Rybak

illustrated by Gary Mohrmann

Cover by Gary Mohrmann

Copyright © Good Apple, 1991

ISBN No. 0-86653-620-5

Printing No. 987654321

Good Apple
1204 Buchanan St., Box 299
Carthage, IL 62321-0299

SIMON & SCHUSTER *A Paramount Communications Company*

Dedication

Over the past few years I have had the opportunity to work as a national educational consultant. During that time I traveled to over forty states and visited with hundreds of teachers. This book is dedicated to all of the wonderful people I met along my journey. Some of you took me to dinner and some took me into your homes. Many people carried my seventy-pound suitcase and a few stayed up late waiting for my plane. I met your teachers and your families. I listened to the stories of your schools and your culture. Although my visit may have been short and our time together brief, you stay in my mind and in my heart. Each act of kindness will forever be appreciated.

I am now back in the classroom doing a job I also love, teaching. But a part of all of you will forever remain with me. Thank you and God bless.

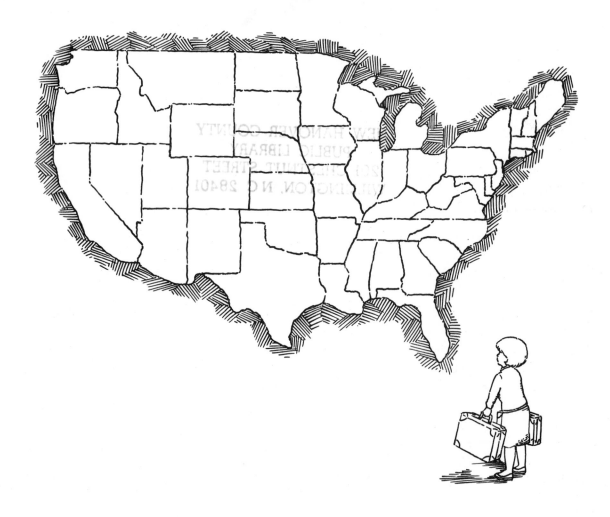

GA1339

Building a Sound Foundation for a Successful Career

GA1339

GA1339

GA1339

Teach Happy, Not Sad
Teach Funny, Not Serious
Teach Higher, Not Lower
Teach Brighter, Not Dimmer
Teach Kinder, Not Harsher
Teach Sooner, Not Later
Teach with Passion, Not Power
Teach Smarter, Not Harder

GA1339

Introduction

There are just some things people never tell you when you start teaching such as how to make friends with the school janitor, how to survive school lunches and what to do with your first angry parent. These are vital components that get left out of education classes.

As a beginning teacher you may feel unsure and have hundreds of what you consider to be *stupid questions*. There is no such thing! This book is designed to answer the questions that you may not even think to ask.

I have included funny stories and bits of advice from fellow teachers whom I have met in my travels as an educational consultant. These terrific folks share their personal points of view on a number of issues. You will notice an owl and A Word from the Wise at the beginning of each of these sections.

The views expressed in this book are mine and also those of my husband, Bob Rybak, who is also a teacher. Together we share over thirty years of teaching experience from kindergarten to college. We discussed many of the sensitive issues and used our joint experiences to share what we considered to be the best possible advice.

Finally, I want to wish all of you a wonderful, successful year and career. You have chosen a difficult, challenging and rewarding profession. Remember that every action you take affects a child. My best wishes to all of you.

GA1339

The Parts and Pieces
of Being a Teacher

GA1339

Your Teaching Style

Over the years every teacher develops his or her own particular teaching style. During the first years of teaching you will begin to formulate your "type" of teaching. Here are a few examples.

The KINESTHETIC Teacher

These teachers are on the move. In general they are people who like movement and learn best when they are actively engaged, so they build that type of classroom for their children. The classroom may be filled with centers and the children may have opportunities to move freely about the classroom. This type of teacher may use movement as a transition between subjects and will be out on the playground jumping rope with the students. They are generally people who are athletic and enjoy sports. This type of teacher will frequently reward students with pats on the back and physical reinforcement.

If you are a kinesthetic teacher, your principal and staff may wonder about the noise coming from your classroom. Movement always equals noise. Quality activities that create learning and teaching noise is good noise. Learn to listen and WATCH the type of noise being created.

The VISUAL Teacher

Have you ever walked into a classroom that is on visual overdose? There are so many things hanging from the ceiling that it looks like a second grade jungle. This is probably a visual teacher who took it one step too far. Visual teachers provide an environment of visual attractions for children. Every lesson is accompanied by some sort of picture, movie, chart, picture book, etc. Visual teachers will frequently use the word *look*.

The AUDITORY Teacher

The auditory teacher will have a classroom that is filled with noise or void of noise. Auditory teachers may like classical music playing in the background or like a quiet classroom where children work in relative silence. These teachers are either attracted or distracted by noise of any kind. They may have listening centers throughout the room and encourage children to work in discussion groups. Auditory teachers frequently use the word *listen*.

GA1339

The CLUTTER Teacher

If the stuff piled up on the top of the piano ever avalanched, the clutter teachers could significantly decrease their class size. Some teachers are messy teachers. Their rooms lack neatness and yet they can always put their hands on something with amazing speed. Having a messy room or a clean room has little, if no reflection on a teacher's ability to teach children. I've been in cluttered rooms with wonderful teachers and neat rooms with not so wonderful teachers and vice versa. Of course the mess should be controlled and should not be a distraction to the children's learning, but some clutter is to be expected.

The NEAT Teacher

If all the children have their boxes of crayons with the colors in rainbow order, beware. Some teachers feel a need to keep the room looking neat which creates a sterile looking classroom. The classroom should have a place for everything and everything in its place, but it should also have some clutter and look like children exist within the four walls. Children make messes, spill paint and leave trails of paper. A room should have order but no obsessive order.

The FUN Teacher

Some teachers are fun teachers. They have always got some wild, fun activities going on in their classrooms. The newspaper reporters and the TV cameras are frequently stopping to marvel at what they will think of next. All of the fun activities are great for children and community relations are very important. Caution: If you're a fun teacher, make sure your fun has clear objectives and expected outcomes. Don't let the excitement of the project lose its teaching value along the way.

The PASSIVE Teacher

Nothing too much happens in the passive teacher's classroom. He/She may have tried those new ideas once and found they didn't work. They keep changing the textbook every few years which means the lesson plans need to be redone again. Teaching is a job. The bulletin boards are the same every year and the children all sort of run together. The children learn, the year passes with a countdown of the number of days that remain.

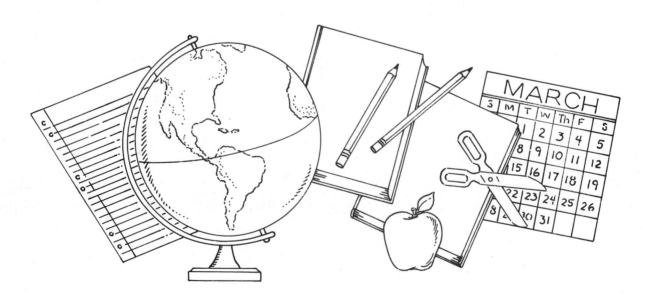

GA1339

All Rolled into One

Each teacher at any particular moment is a part of each of the "teacher types" listed. Sometimes we are on the move with our children and enjoy getting up and dancing with them. On some days we can't believe it's only 1:30 p.m. There are some days when we can't stand to hear our own name and others where we don't notice the noise until our neighbor teacher closes our door loudly. Sometimes we can't find our desk and other times the room has incredible organization. There is the day before Christmas break when it's a pleasure to remove all the decorations and days when you can't think of one good idea to display.

The point is that your classroom is a dynamic environment. In definition *dynamic* means "powerful forces not in equilibrium." A classroom is sort of like a train ride. Passengers get on and off the train, and the scenery is always changing. The train moves fast and sometimes very slowly. It even occasionally comes to a complete stop. It makes loud noise and carries all types of cargo. The conductor calls, "All aboard" and the teacher journeys through the next nine months with his/her passengers.

To have a dynamic classroom, teachers need to go with the flow of the children on a particular trip. The destination might be the same, but some years the road is steep and difficult over the mountain pass. To have dynamic classrooms, teachers must adjust their styles to meet the needs of the children in their classrooms.

So be prepared to move if some children need to move; enjoy the movement with them. Provide the visual for those children that are reinforced by sight. Remember that some children respond to noise, and others are distracted by noise. Keep a healthy balance.

Don't compare your classroom with those of other teachers. They are on another trip with different passengers. Your trip is unique to the individuals you have been entrusted to teach. If you have children who love mess but from their mess show great creativity and original thought, go with the mess. If you have children who love mess just to mess, build on the structure. Remember this is a dynamic place that is always changing, especially you. If you don't like change and new situations, this isn't the right profession. It is said teachers teach the ways in which THEY learn. To create a dynamic classroom, teachers must always teach in the ways CHILDREN learn.

GA1339

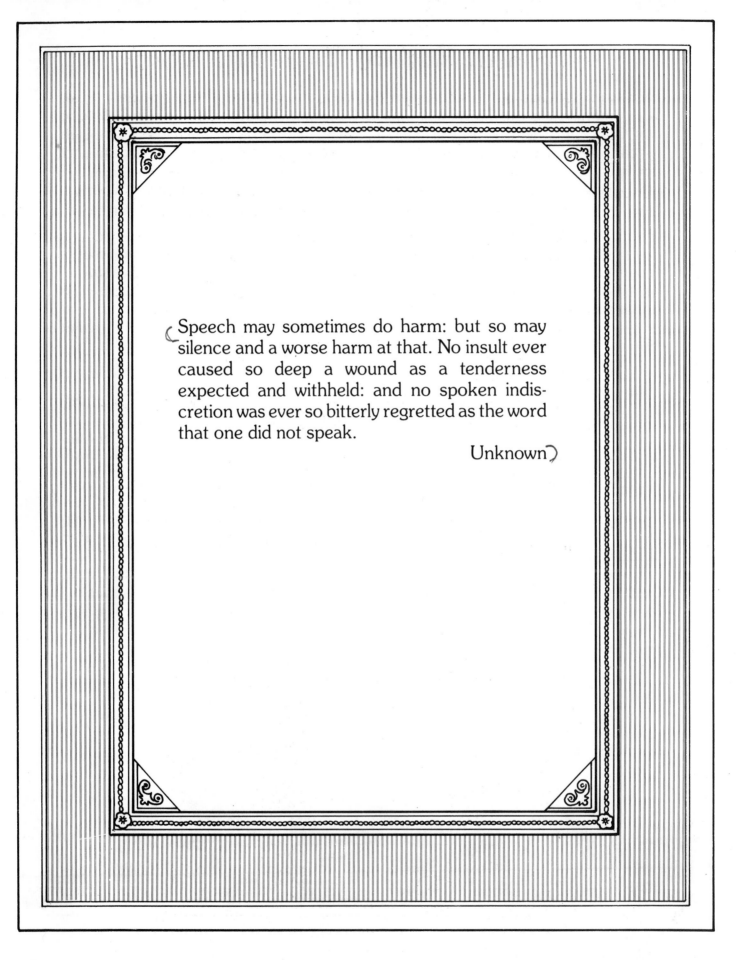

Speech may sometimes do harm: but so may silence and a worse harm at that. No insult ever caused so deep a wound as a tenderness expected and withheld: and no spoken indiscretion was ever so bitterly regretted as the word that one did not speak.

Unknown

GA1339

Developing Your Teacher Voice

When traveling alone through Chicago one evening, I found myself in line between two men in the baggage claim area. The two men began to argue over the position of their bags, and the argument quickly escalated to shoves and very loud yelling. Suddenly from deep inside me a VERY assertive voice said, "That will be enough, gentlemen! I have other ways to spend my evening than to tolerate this behavior. I suggest you stop it immediately." I was so startled at myself that I hardly thought about what I had just done. Immediately they stopped and the wife of the one man quickly pulled him away.

From my recesses I had pulled my "teacher voice." It said, in no uncertain terms, "stop!" That incident made me reflect on the impact that voice of mine has had over the years. It's not a yell or a scream or even loud. Sometimes it's even soft, but it always comes from deep within me. And that is the key. Whenever you talk to children, talk from your heart, really mean what you say.

You will use your teacher voice to get attention, to teach a lesson, to discipline, to reward, to acknowledge, to warn, to soothe. Some people talk to children in sarcastic tones and yet use kind words. Children know words not spoken from the heart.

Some people yell at children. When you yell, children quickly learn not to pay attention until you begin yelling. Some teachers have a difficult time with inflection. The studies show that most people "tune out" after about five minutes, so teachers need to develop an interesting voice that holds children's attention.

One of the best training grounds for teachers is to become involved in the art of storytelling. Storytelling, without a book, forces you to center your attention on the delivery of the words to communicate the story. Great storytellers have truly magical voices!

Part of your teaching repertoire should be a voice that fits the situation and always comes from the heart.

7

GA1339

Other Teachers as Role Models

"To the left of me was the Grinch and across the hall was a Mrs. Mary Sunshine." This is how one teacher described her first year of collaborative teaching. "One teacher encouraged me to open up with the children; the other thought I was too lax. It was hard to carve out my own identity as a teacher."

The process of teaching, student interaction, demeanor, response time, pacing and so many other teacher interpersonal interactions require practice and observation of other teachers. Good teaching is an art form. Teachers who can engage their students with what appears to be minimal effort and have a positive attitude with their students is much more difficult than it looks.

That first year is also filled with questions and concerns over policy and procedures. Those questions and directions are usually answered by our teaching peers. Carefully choose the teacher you wish to use as a resource and possibly as a role model.

Frequently the teacher we will become involved with is our partner teacher(s) on that grade level. If you are not comfortable with that teacher's demeanor toward children or philosophy, keep looking throughout the building for another teacher who will help lead you through the process. Don't be afraid to admit that you're looking for a mentor.

Many schools have mentor programs for their new teachers to help them traverse the ropes. School is more than teaching curriculum. Each school has policies, special programs, committees and a variety of other specifics that you have to learn through experience. It's comforting to have someone who will entertain your questions in an open and honest fashion.

8

Collaboration

As a new teacher you may be surprised by how alone you are in your classroom. If you are in an open classroom setting, you may have the opportunity to see and hear your fellow teachers interacting with their students. Most teachers, however, are teaching in a classroom with a door that closes them off to the other children and other teachers. It is important to establish a collaboration between yourself and your fellow teachers to break down the isolation of your classroom.

As a teacher you need to keep track of your fellow teachers' pace on the curriculum. Be informed about curriculum that is taught by other teachers the year before and the year that follows your grade level. It may also be valuable to gather information about particular students so you will be better able to service their needs. Be careful not to fall into the trap of teachers who are overly anxious to share only negative information about children.

In a collaborative group, teachers share ideas, philosophy, information, resources, positive assurance and confirmation. You may be entering your profession with a great deal of enthusiasm and excitement. You may be ready to take on the world. Don't forget that your partner teachers may not be ready for that pace, and that may not be a negative reflection on their ability to teach. They may move with a slower, steadier pace but with a sure hand. You may be like that new puppy with a little too much energy. Be careful not to wear everyone down with excitement, but do bring your new ideas and share within a comfortable time frame.

Don't be afraid to ask. Seek the knowledge you need to do the job well. If you have a question about a child, go to last year's teacher for an answer. If you want to develop a unit, ask other teachers for direction. Almost all teachers are flattered and enjoy helping a new teacher. Seek out the collaborative group.

GA1339

Children Will Respond to Our Faces Before They Will Respond to Our Words

The first thing children notice is the teacher's face. When you are angry, they will be able to tell by your eyes and your expressions. Children are very adept at reading people's faces and bypassing their words. I personally think that is because as young children they don't understand many conversations but study faces to gather meaning.

If you say one thing and mean another, children can tell. Children can quickly identify those people who like children and are sincere. Don't ever underestimate children's ability to read people.

How does this affect us as teachers? We can move children and motivate them toward certain tasks through the use of our facial expression. Giving children sincere eye contact and smiles is one sure way to get their attention. Teachers can also wink, grin, make faces and create hundreds of facial expressions that encourage and help the child feel connected.

Constipated Smiles

Don't give children your "teacher" smile. These are usually accompanied by some verbal nonsense that sounds like teacher blabber. These phony smiles are as sincere as those chimed good mornings by the entire class, "Good morningggggg, Mrs. Rybaaaaaak!"

If you look closely you will discover the child within you. It is the same child who enjoys a good giggle, who responds to some positive recognition and enjoys people who enjoy themselves and act *real*. That is the teacher who you want to be and the person your children will learn from and respect.

Never forget that within you rests a child who has just outgrown his/her clothes. Find the child and you will find the best teacher you can be!

GA1339

Take Care of Yourself

A Word from the Wise

Trudy Sampugnaro
St. Andrew Apostle School
Principal
Maryland

Get a lot of rest! I was never so tired or so sick as I was that first year of teaching. Since that time I've watched many new teachers begin their careers, and they only do as well as their last good night's sleep.

This is wonderful advice from a wonderful lady. Teachers need to feel on top of the world so they can stay on top of the class! Your lack of sleep or poor health robs you of one of your most important attributes as a teacher, your patience.

Most germs are passed by hands so make sure you wash your hands frequently, especially after grading papers and before lunch. Try to keep your hands away from your face and mouth.

If the children begin to come down with a wave of illness, ask that their desks be washed and the room disinfected. Little units on hand washing, using tissues and blowing noses may also help the cause.

Finally, give yourself time to relax as well as sleep. Teachers will be better prepared if they have some relaxing family time and social fun. Having a good mental attitude is one of your best lines of defense against illness and exhaustion.

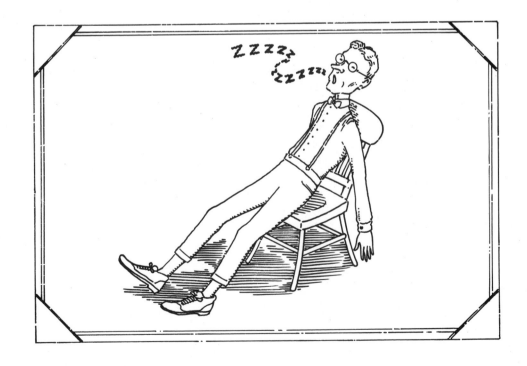

Ignorance Is Bliss

During your first year as a teacher you move through the year with calm assurance. OK, maybe not so calm, but first-year teachers rarely feel pressure to get it all done because they are only beginning to realize how much could actually be done or needs to be done.

I think one of the biggest stress points for all teachers is the diversity of needs within one classroom. As a new teacher you may begin to realize that this job could be workable if the ratio was one teacher to ten children. When one teacher has close to thirty children with a variety of needs, the job may seem overwhelming.

Teachers also want to fully implement new ideas and expect to have the innovation totally in place in a short period of time. We put great demands on our energy trying to be super teachers.

The first year may be one of the best years because you can move with relative ease and feel comfortable in the role of novice. Enjoy it while it lasts.

A Word from the Wise

Jo Ann Bowman
Lancaster Independent School District
Assistant Principal
Texas

I have been in the "school business" now for twenty-six years. The last six of them have not been in the classroom. There are so many things to be learned outside the college classroom. I remember the first time I taught second grade handwriting. As a new teacher I had not taken the time (nor had I had the time) to see what was being taught the year before. I was beginning to teach cursive writing, and I passed out regular notebook paper to the students and began my lesson. I had given no thought to the fact that the children had not been using lined paper and writing much larger than a single line of paper would allow. I "expected" the students to do this, and, fortunately, they did. As I later learned I could have made it easier for all of us had I realized that I was not teaching in a vacuum. My advice is to listen to experience, but attempt to always keep that fresh feeling of enthusiasm that new teachers bring to education.

Another thing that I would suggest would be to read the book *Christy* by Catherine Marshall. The first year of teaching is a busy, hectic time in one's life, and there is little time for reading for pleasure alone. This is one book that puts things in perspective. I have read it countless times and I am sure I will do so again.

GA1339

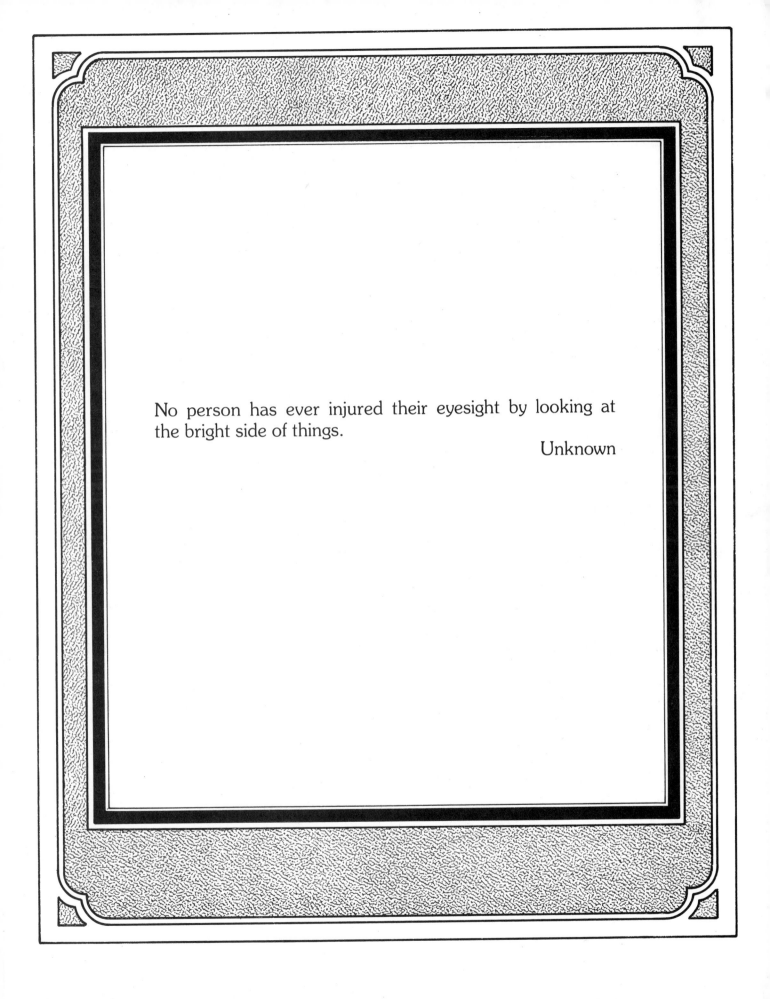

No person has ever injured their eyesight by looking at the bright side of things.

Unknown

GA1339

Lounge Lizards and Other Dangerous Animals

Lounge lizards is a term used for teachers who dwell in faculty lounges. *Dwell* is the operative word. They dwell on negative behaviors; they dwell on what they don't like; they dwell on parents they don't like, and of course they dwell on the administrators they don't like.

Lounge lizards can turn happy, sunny teachers into crabby, unhappy teachers if they spend too much time with this breed.

It is important to build a rapport with your staff, and frequently the lounge is one of the few places where you meet and talk. If you have lounge lizards, try a few tactics for changing the subject or inviting a few teachers to walk during lunch. A Friday pot-luck lunch might be a way to change the subject and tone of lunch.

Many schools now have separate lounges for smokers and nonsmokers. If you are a smoker, make sure you spend time visiting with the nonsmokers and vice versa.

Be cautious when you talk to certain teachers who seem to look for gossip. A comment made in the faculty room can come back to haunt you if that information is repeated to the wrong person. Even innocent remarks can be misquoted. Always try to keep your remarks positive and do your talking to a trusted colleague or your principal.

GA1339

Surviving School Lunches

School lunch becomes boring. Having to pack a lunch or buy a school lunch is fine for the first month, and after that it becomes a hassle. I always laugh at older teachers who have whittled lunch down to a grapefruit or an apple. It's just easier.

Don't pack a big lunch for yourself. After eating a big lunch your body will use its energy for digestion of that big meal. You need your energy to deal with a group of children who have just popped off the blacktop playground. Things don't work well if your children are ready for action, and you're ready for a nap.

Try to pack for the week. Your mornings will be busy and most of us are lucky to get to school with makeup on both sides of our faces and no runs in the stockings, or for the gentlemen matching socks and a shave. Packing a nutritious lunch may not work into the plan. Most schools have some sort of refrigerators for teachers, and things store in your school refrigerator as well as your home refrigerator. For example, if you make tuna fish for yourself, take enough for a few days and take some crackers and a piece of cheese. Pack fruit and eat the most perishable fruit first. If you like variety, try making your sandwiches for the week and freezing them. Most brands of lunch meat do very well, but save the condiments until you're ready for lunch.

Encourage other teachers to start a Friday salad bar where everyone brings one component of the bar. A staff of 256 teachers can put on a beautiful salad bar with little individual effort. Order out from a deli on occasion and have it delivered to the school if you have a short lunch hour. Another fun group lunch is a baked potato bar. Every teacher brings a component of the potato bar, and the potatoes are cooked in the cafeteria ovens in the morning.

Although teaching is a very tiring profession, it does not use up a lot of calories. Be careful not to begin having snacks at every break and treats for every birthday. Most new teachers gain weight and are exhausted at the same time. It seems impossible to be working so hard and yet gaining weight.

Be creative with your lunch and don't turn Gummy Bears into a food group.

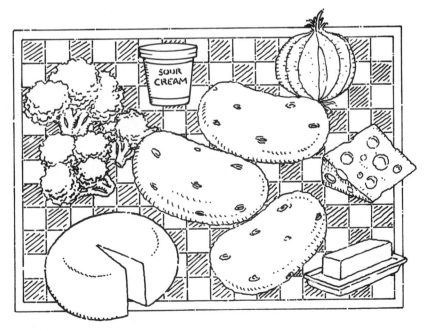

GA1339

Taking Work Home

The first bit of garbage you will receive as a teacher is how short your day is, how much time you get off at Christmas and a three-month vacation in the summer. These people need to see you at 11:30 Sunday evening when you are still preparing your lessons for the next week.

Teachers have a chronic problem of working at home. The school day seldom provides the kind of time necessary to develop well-planned and executed lessons. Taking work home is just another part of the unwritten job description.

If at all possible look for an extra set of classroom manuals for the different textbook series and keep the set at home during the school year. This will give you a chance to do the work without breaking your back carrying manuals home.

Enlist the services of as many parents as possible for special projects. Don't take on the collection of all the milk cartons or decorations for Grandparents' Day. Your time should be spent on lesson preparation and curriculum development and not on cutting out letters.

Some teachers spend every spare moment working on some sort of school project. Although this shows great dedication, it is one sure way to burn out on teaching. I talk from experience. One summer I made every game for my classroom that was imaginable. My excitement wore off about November, and I found I did not have my reserve energy. Everyone needs a break and time away from the demanding job of teaching.

Creating Your Room Environment

GA1339

Where Do I Start?

"Well, Miss Brown, this is your room, number 107. You will find your books in the cupboard area and your supplies will be passed out at the first faculty meeting. Last year's teacher has left the teacher's manuals in the top left-hand drawer. If you have any questions, I'll be in the office most of the day."

That's it? Don't leave. Where do I begin? Those first few moments in your first classroom are so exciting and scary. How do I turn these four walls into a classroom? It reminds me of some of the feelings I had when I brought my first child home from the hospital. I got the job; the excitement is over; now it's time to get down to work.

Start with the physical environment, and do what you can do first and move to the more impossible tasks later. Count the desks and the number of children you expect to have. Always plan on five extra that will come along during the year. Move the desks or tables in a variety of ways to see how they fit in the room. Try some original designs and remember that it will all be changed once school begins; it's a dynamic environment.

Try to add some of your own personal touches to the room. A rocking chair and small rug is my personal favorite. You might want a director's chair or an old trunk. Some teachers like a teaching stool or a lamp in the room. Whatever you choose, make it something that gives the room warmth and a comfortable feeling.

The physical space also includes the sights and sounds within the classroom. Don't turn desks toward windows or place children too close to doors. Try to keep the distractions to a minimum. Think about the flow of traffic to lockers or hooks, the pencil sharpener, the bathroom, chalkboards and other areas.

A Word from the Wise

Mr. Ray Horvath
Principal
Farmington, New Mexico

1988 New Mexico State
Principal of the Year

My memories go back to 67 children in a classroom with 35 chairs and no books. My supplies for the year were three packages of newsprint that probably cost 35 cents per ream. Our ditto machine was the gelatin type of machine where one could make one copy at a time. My smallest class was 40 students. If we couldn't handle discipline, it was tough. We got no support from the principal. Staff meetings were always upsetting. If one teacher did something wrong, we were all criticized for the offense. Most of the time we never knew why we had the staff meeting. It was 35 years before I was ever evaluated. Have times changed?

Classroom Space

Some teachers have rooms so large they need roller skates and others have classrooms the size of closets. Many specialists do teach in closets.

One of the major complaints is space to display work, develop centers or store materials. Some teachers have found some unusual and unique solutions for these problems.

Lattice used for an outdoor trellis can be hinged together to make a divider that can be seen through. Artwork easily hangs from the wooden crossbars and the children can also use this for center activities.

A tree branch can be suspended from the ceiling and makes a wonderful display area for three-dimensional art projects. It can also become a center with task cards attached with colorful clothespins to each branch.

Large cardboard display boards can be purchased from most teacher stores. These allow the teacher to develop the center and display it on a table or floor. When the center is done, it can be safely stored for the next year.

Shoe box storage units also work well for children's materials or mailboxes.

Take an Outsider's View

As you walk into your classroom, try to take an outsider's view of what he sees as he enters. Is there clutter near the door, or is it organized? Does the environment look welcoming and like a place you would like to stay and visit? Are there items of interest and things that any individual would enjoy exploring? Is the light bright and yet not blinding, and is the organization of the room good for movement from place to place? Do people question what things are and say, "That looks interesting"? Is there a place for a quiet moment to read or reflect? Do you want to spend your day in this room, and do the children you teach want to spend their day here as well?

I Like This Classroom

Here are a few other things that will bring life to your classroom.

Pictures	Live animals such as:
Paintings	snails
Plants	rabbits
Wind chimes	ant farms
Kaleidoscopes	hamsters
Photographs	guinea pigs
Posters	birds
Beanbag chairs	
Old bathtub	

Remember to put everything at the eye level of the children you are teaching. Don't go for too much or too little on the walls. Leave space for them to take ownership of the room.

Create a soft place where children can relax. Children come from homes with couches and beds and pillows, and we throw them into hard desks for eight hours. All of us head for our favorite soft spot at the end of a long day, and children also need a comfortable space for retreating occasionally.

Make sure your room has things that are touchable. Children need to have things around that they are allowed to touch, even big children. Look at the popularity of stores and museums that allow people to touch. It's a basic need. Provide old telephones that are half taken apart, motors, beautiful rocks and crystals or anything that looks fun to explore. Everything does not need to have a behavioral objective, because some materials can be provided for their own merit or value.

GA1339

Start a Collection

Collectors are fun people. They are always on the lookout for some inexpensive items that will add to their collections of goodies. The funniest one I have ever heard of was the lady who collected samples of toilet paper (clean) whenever she traveled. She wrote the place she got it and the date. Well, I don't suggest that you and your children collect toilet paper, but collections can be good learning tools for classification, reading, organization and research. Here are a few examples.

stones and rocks	cartoons	old or new magazines
pencils	stamps	receipts
football pins	foreign coins	different seeds
funny sayings	rulers	animal pictures

The possibilities are endless. Stamp collectors need to research the various countries, and are involved in math computations. Studying football teams is a good way to teach states and cities. Teach math by keeping statistics on each team. Keep your collection going for the entire year and get everyone involved.

Become Experts

Follow the general nature of teaching and watch for something that is of particular appeal to your students. Take that subject area and become experts. Experts are authorities in a particular field. Tell the other students in the building that you have become experts and will be happy to help them if they ever study that area. Your children may want to become experts about dinosaurs, volcanoes or experts about your home state. You may only have a few children who want to study one area and others who are interested in something else. Make sure that you are learning along with the children. This is not the time to be the teacher but the time to be the learner. The teacher models the act of being inquisitive.

These kinds of activities create a feeling of unity in a classroom. The children demonstrate group cooperation and the feeling of a common goal. When the teacher learns with the students, the teacher becomes an insider and is one of the learners. Children get a feeling for emersion into a subject area and a sense of a common mission.

Rules: Everyone must be able to contribute.
      Let the project evolve from the children.
      Teachers should not take ownership.
      The project belongs to everyone.

GA1339

Bulletin Boards, Commercial Material and Children's Work

A great deal of the classroom environment is created on the bulletin boards. They project the areas studied and provide color and excitement to the classroom. Many commercial materials are available that are fun and add decoration to a classroom. The problem is that commercial materials alone leave a classroom looking just that—commercial. The personal touches are absent in a room that relies solely on store-bought materials.

But what if you are not artistic and have trouble putting up backing paper and a border? Here are some suggestions.

- Find pictures of characters that you would like on your bulletin board and make an overhead of the character on the copy machine.
- Trace the overhead design on a large piece of paper.
- Children can color or paint on the design. I have even done this with four and five-year-olds.
- Have the children do different parts of the bulletin board such as some children make the clouds, others the flowers, some the house and a few children make the trees.
- Start with a character such as a teddy bear and have each child make a bear. Let the children develop a community for the bears with playgrounds, schools and houses. This works for any community, zoo or farm unit.
- One bulletin board should belong to the children, and they should create a board that reflects their interests from sports to movies, etc. This can be done by committees of three people. The teacher may need to give them a title to get them started. Give them deadlines as to when it must be completed.
- "Doing boards" is the most fun for students because they can learn and be involved and not be in their seats! They can create a matching board such as match the space of the state to its name, or a gameboard with questions that need to have researched answers. Children can put the answers in their journals, and the answers can be revealed on Friday. Children can frequently help with the creation of these boards.
- The pride wall is a place in the classroom where children get to select their best work and place it on the wall. Empty frames can also be placed on the wall and children can put their best pictures in the frames.

22

GA1339

Before You Meet the Students

GA1339

Overview the Curriculum

There is a variety of sources available to the teacher when making decisions about curriculum content and the order in which that curriculum should be taught. It is very important to get a clear picture of the expectations for the children and the pacing for you as the teacher.

- Most states mandate that individual school districts have curriculum standards that will be taught for each grade level. In most cases these are *minimum* standards and may not reflect the expectation for the individual children.
- Make sure to ask for the district curriculum standards for your grade level assignment. Some of the objectives will be introduced while others are expected to be taught for mastery.
- The front of most teaching manuals has a scope and sequence chart that covers the content areas for each grade level and also a content overview for that particular grade's curriculum.
- The scope and sequence chart lays out what came before your particular grade and what will come in following grades.
- Look for areas of the curriculum that will dovetail into each other, for example, a unit on math story problems tied in with creative writing or history with a literature book. This not only helps the children learn in context, it also saves teaching time and allows the subjects to flow.
- Always keep your teaching objectives close at hand and make reference to them during the school year. It is important to know where you are going and the time it will take to get there.

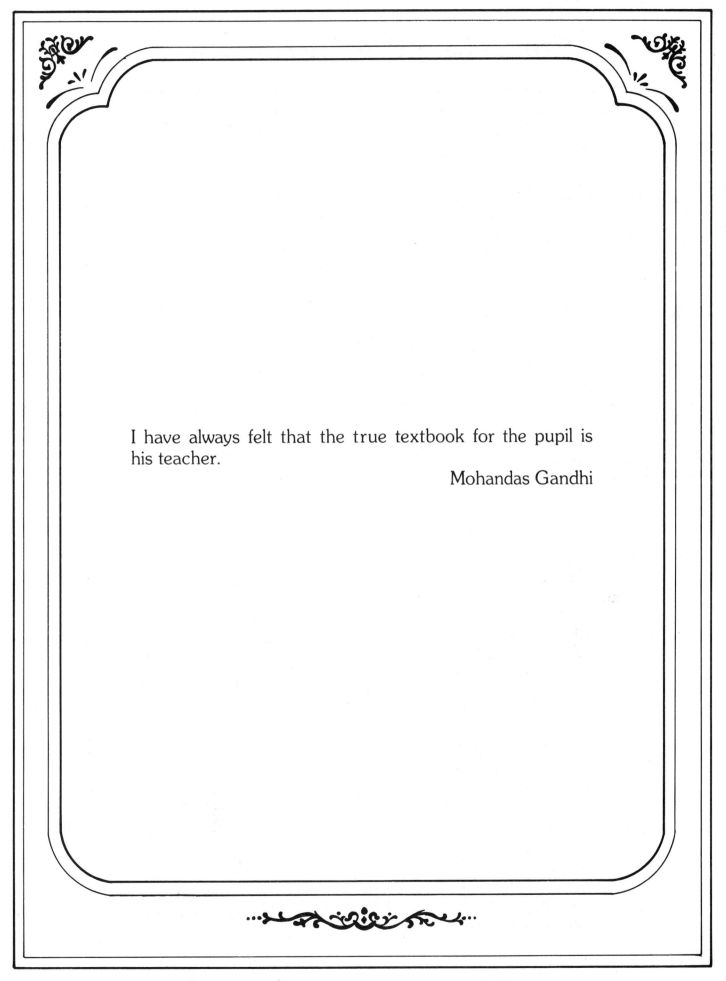

I have always felt that the true textbook for the pupil is his teacher.

Mohandas Gandhi

Pacing Your Year

The subject content overview format on the next page is taken from the *Good Apple Lesson Organizer*. It is designed to be filled in by the teacher at the beginning of the school year for each subject area. As the areas are filled in, watch for subjects that would compliment each other and try to organize the subject areas into the units or look for themes that can be developed.

CAUTION: The saying "ignorance is bliss" really fits in this situation. Once teachers realize all that needs to be introduced, developed or mastered, the year can seem overwhelming and teaching becomes a race to the finish line. Remember that the most important element of a classroom is always the children. They need to feel comfortable and confident about learning, not rushed and always behind. The student's self-concept is as important as the teaching of the curriculum.

Subject: Content Overview — *Social Studies*

September	October	November	December	January
GEOGRAPHY REVIEW AND MAP READING UNIT 1 pp. 11-77	FIRST AMERICANS AND EXPLORERS UNIT 2 & 3 pp. 129-204	LIFE IN THE COLONIES: LEAD UP TO AMERICAN REVOLUTION UNIT 4-5 pp. 204-263 REPORT/PROJECT ON COLONIAL LIFE	THE AMERICAN REVOLUTION UNIT 5 pp. 263-293 (only 2½ weeks this month)	DEVELOPMENT OF THE CONSTITUTION AND THE LOUISIANA PURCHASE UNIT 6 pp. 295-333 SPECIAL THREE-DAY UNIT ON MARTIN LUTHER KING

February	March	April	May	June
FOCUS ON PRESIDENTS: PROJECT/REPORT ON ONE OF THE PRESIDENTS DUE BY FEB. 16th. WESTWARD EXPANSION TRANSPORTATION GOLD RUSH pp. 334-360	WESTWARD EXPANSION SOUTHWEST pp. 361-370 CAUSES OF CIVIL WAR & CIVIL WAR BATTLES UNIT 7 pp. 371-415	CONCLUDE CIVIL WAR IF NECESSARY RECONSTRUCTION AND INDUSTRIAL AGE UNIT 8 pp. 417-443	FOCUS ON INVENTORS PROJECT - CREATE AN INVENTION UNIT 8 pp. 443-463 IMMIGRATION AND WWI UNIT 9 pp. 465-483	MODERN TIMES WWII - PRESENT UNIT 9 483-512

GA1339

Subject: Content Overview

September	October	November	December	January

February	March	April	May	June

What Are Your Goals?

Every year starts with resolutions of things that would like to be done, such as develop two new units and ten new charts or build poetry into the reading curriculum. It may be certain units that will be developed around the science or social studies curriculum. As a new teacher it may be difficult to predict what personal touches you would like to develop into the curriculum. The benefits of making decisions about the units early is that it gives you, as the teacher, "collection time." If you plan early that a dinosaur unit is perfect for your class, then your eyes will be wide open to "dinosaur stuff." Collection of quality materials that will supplement a unit takes planning and time.

If you have a particular area of interest or expertise, make sure to build that into your school year. Share your love of a particular subject or collection with your children. Include a personal dimension of your life into a classroom unit. Here are a few examples: a friend who loves sailing—read books about sailing and use the terms from sailing for spelling lessons, diagram boats and spend one day sailing on the lake. Antiques from various periods are a wonderful leadoff for an exciting history unit. A wonderful cook used a unit on baking to begin the measurement unit.

A teacher's own unique presentation of the curriculum makes teaching fun and interesting for the teacher and the children.

GA1339

Setting the Stage

As the children enter the classroom on the first day, they should recognize their place in that classroom. The best way to do that is to place their names on desks, bulletin boards, doors or walls. Children love to see their names, and it makes them feel welcome.

Plan ahead for organization of the child's material and their demands for space. Children don't share well when their space is invaded and crowded locker areas and mailbox traffic invite conflicts. Muddy boots, lost and found, wet art projects, science equipment and lost crayons all need special attention.

Paper—Paper—Paper—Paper—Paper

One of the largest organizational problems teachers face is paper management. Even with the diminished use of dittos, children still record their responses, write stories and keep journals. Some teachers have the children keep files or portfolios of their work for a period of time before sending the work home. Other teachers keep mailboxes and have the children take their work home daily. Another strategy is to have work taken home every Friday.

When children hand in their work they need to place their completed products in baskets, shelves or mailboxes. Student helpers can check off the work as it is handed in. Children can also check off their names as work is completed or the teacher can keep personal records of students' completed work. This can become an overwhelming task if it becomes involved and too intricate. Develop an organizational system that is efficient and open that easily monitors the flow of paper through your classroom.

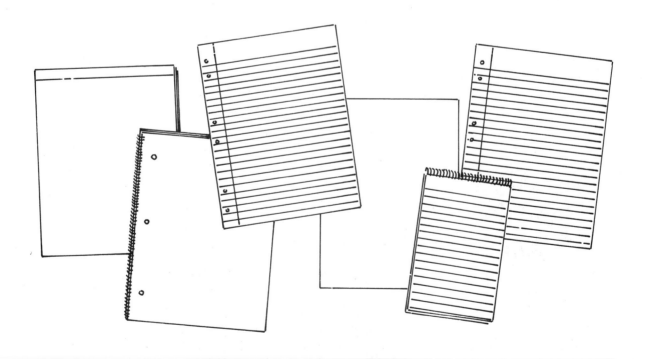

GA1339

The Art of Instruction

30

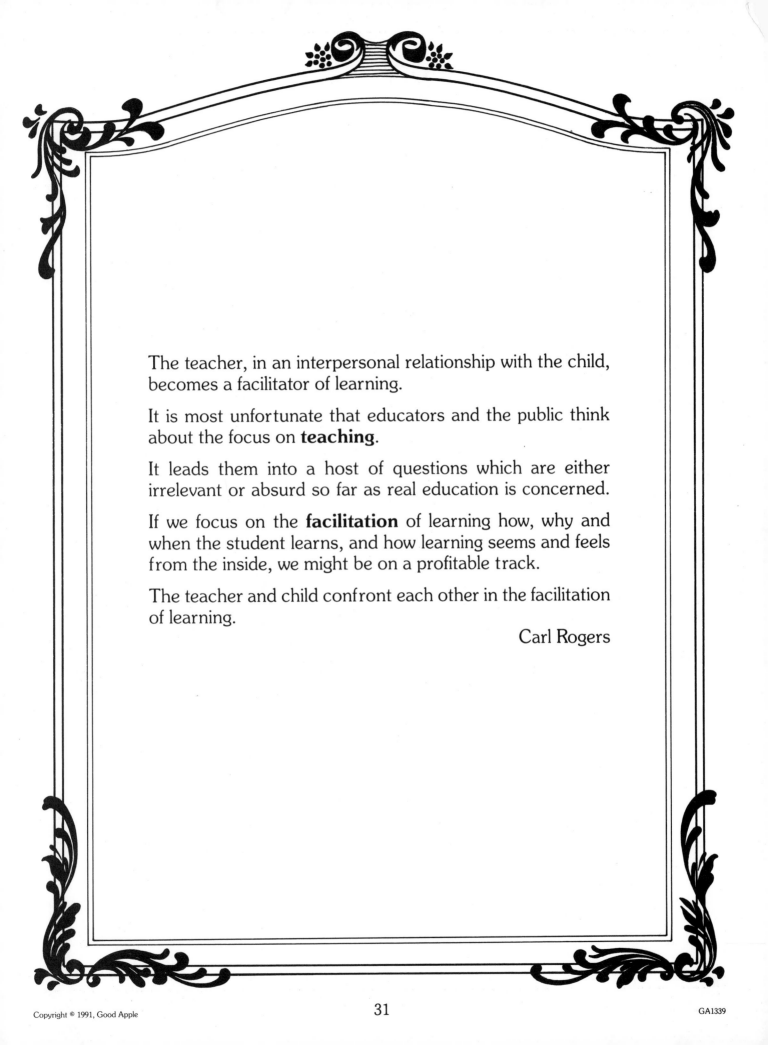

The teacher, in an interpersonal relationship with the child, becomes a facilitator of learning.

It is most unfortunate that educators and the public think about the focus on **teaching**.

It leads them into a host of questions which are either irrelevant or absurd so far as real education is concerned.

If we focus on the **facilitation** of learning how, why and when the student learns, and how learning seems and feels from the inside, we might be on a profitable track.

The teacher and child confront each other in the facilitation of learning.

Carl Rogers

GA1339

Teaching and Facilitating

Teaching

When we think of teaching, we get an image of a teacher standing before a group of children with chalk in hand. The teacher talks to the children and the children listen and ask questions. That is the oldest form of instruction and the one that is most familiar. That strategy works well when sharing lessons with the entire group of students, but it is only one of the strategies teachers need to use for successful instruction.

Facilitating

The other teaching strategies fall under what I call facilitating. Each one of these involves the student taking some control of the learning process. Many of these have become teaching buzz words over the past few years, but they all add up to allowing children an opportunity to take ownership for their educational process.

Cooperative learning is a strategy where children work in groups. Each member of the group has ownership to the content, and children are encouraged to work together toward the final product. The teacher acts as the facilitator providing leadership but not as the sole source of information.

Dyads are children that work in groups of two. The teacher carefully matches the children so a comfortable working relationship may be productive for both students. This strategy works well for reading and math instruction.

Each one teach one is a strategy where each participant in the group is responsible for a component of the chapter or unit. Each child then gathers the information and teaches the other group members or the entire class.

Learning centers are designed by the teacher but allow the children to work at an independent pace at activities that support the ongoing curriculum. Children may be held responsible for completing certain tasks that are outlined at each center.

These are only a few of the strategies that get children working together and taking control for their learning.

GA1339

People learn by doing, and direct teaching doesn't allow much opportunity to do anything but listen. Teachers need to step back and discover ways to get children actively involved in the curriculum, using a variety of strategies. Using these strategies can be unsettling for teachers because they force us to loosen our control, and they create some disorder in the learning process. Our ultimate goal as teachers is to give children an ownership for their education and make them lifelong learners. Lifelong learners like to learn and feel empowered to learn.

These are strategies that help children take ownership for the learning process.

Knowing the Goals

Imagine you are on a train ride moving through the countryside seeing lots of interesting sights along the way. The people on the train are fun and you enjoy their company, but you have no idea where the train is going or the final destination. Millions of children are on this train, and they have no idea where they are going or why they are on the train in the first place. The only goal young children know is that they want to learn to read and most do learn to read. After that goal is accomplished, most children don't have established learning goals.

Children respond to goals. Teachers need to share their teaching objectives with children so the child can take ownership for the final product and be encouraged to reach the goal.

> Adult college students are the funniest when it comes to knowing the objectives and the goals for a college level class. They will pin the teacher down on the exact specifications of the course and the expectations for papers and tests. They want to know what chapters need to be read and what articles need to be gathered. These students respond to the goals, but many times the motivation is the grade and not the learning that is taking place.

Daily Goals—Weekly Goals—Monthly Goals—Yearly Goals

As a kindergarten teacher I would ask my children every morning, "Why are you here?" They would answer, "We're here to learn." The first teaching objective of the day was established. Children need to see where the teacher is headed. If it's written on the chalkboard, in the journals, on a sheet of paper in their desks or in a notebook, children need to be keeping track of their progress and working toward learning goals.

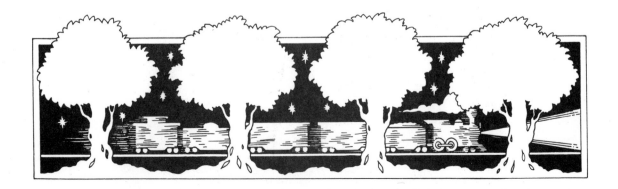

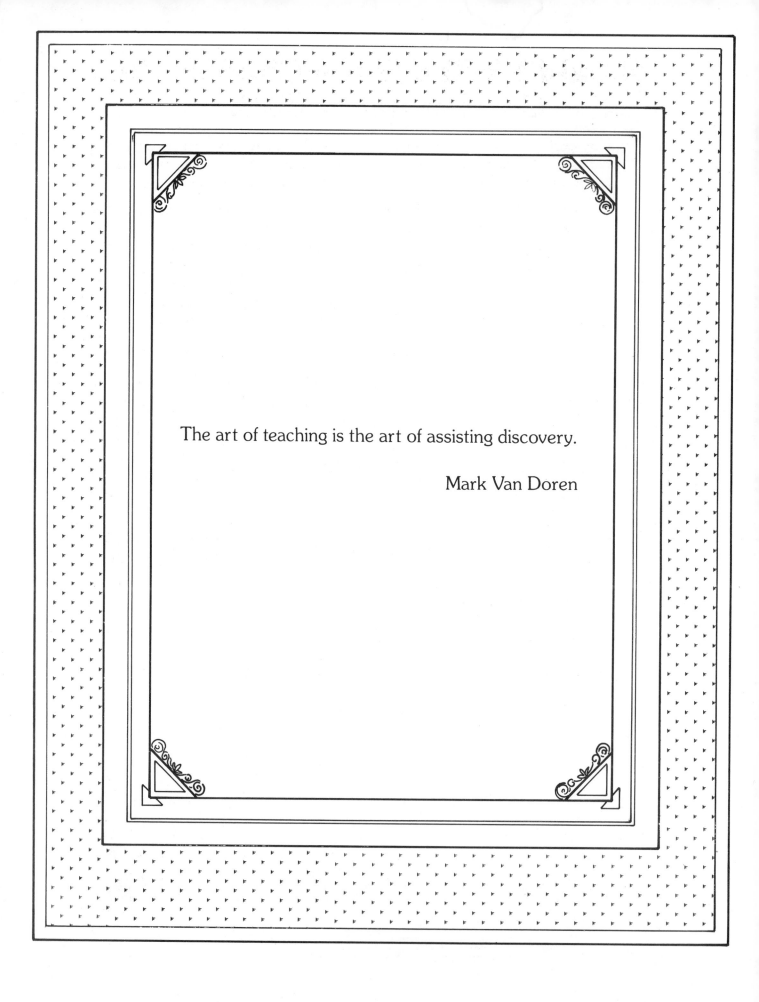

The art of teaching is the art of assisting discovery.

Mark Van Doren

GA1339

Should We Teach the Child or the Curriculum or Both?

This is the age-old question in educational philosophy, "How do we meet the needs of the individual and still move everyone toward a common goal?" I truly believe that the answer rests with the heart and soul of the teacher rather than the mind of the teacher.

In a typical classroom the teacher is always going to have a wide diversity of skill levels, abilities and interests displayed by the children. The teacher is also going to have volumes of material that need to be covered during the course of the school year. This looks like a problem that can be solved by logical, analytical planning and strategy building. That is exactly how many teachers tackle the problem, and it works pretty well, except for those children who don't fit into a logical strategy. These children confuse our logic and do some things well and others poorly. They may have poor self-esteem or motor coordination problems. They may be discipline problems or demand constant attention. They do not fit our well-planned program.

This is where the heart and soul of the teacher steps in and begins to teach the child rather than the curriculum. Outstanding organization and planning are just the beginning of a good teacher's classroom strategy for working with children. The exemplary teacher goes past the curriculum and looks into the eyes of each individual child, watching his/ her growth and development. If you are a new teacher, it is essential that you take time to observe your children. Watch them on the playground, at their desks, in line and at lunch. Learn about their home lives and their likes and dislikes. Watch each child to see what triggers a reaction or generates a smile.

It is possible to teach both the curriculum and the child, but one must not be sacrificed for the other. It is the balance between these two that creates outstanding education.

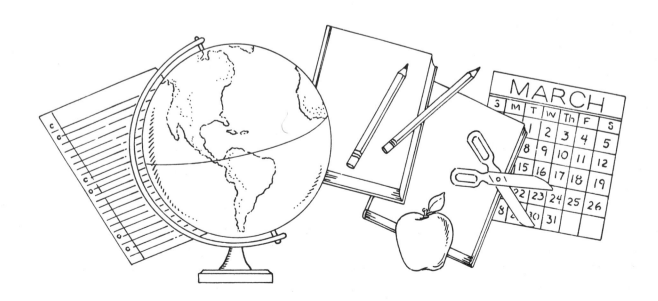

GA1339

Concrete Through Abstract Instruction

Abstract Instruction

Abstract instruction is the easiest to identify. It requires direct recall of information and gives little visual, auditory or kinesthetic support to the student. An example of abstract instruction is a math workbook page of multiplication problems or a series of history questions. Abstract instruction usually comes at the end of a unit or instructional cycle and is frequently used during assessment.

Concrete Instruction

Concrete instruction is a teaching strategy that gives a great deal of visual, auditory or kinesthetic support to the learner. It also provides instruction that is successful for most learners. An example might be math manipulatives used in a game situation. A play that dramatizes an historical event might be another example.

Semi-Concrete Instruction

This is the bridge between abstract and concrete. During this stage there may be supports in the visual, auditory and kinesthetic, but there also may be a need for recall and application on the part of the learner. An example might be math story problems where children are encouraged to use manipulatives to create the situation. A history lesson with pictures that need to be put in sequence might be another example.

The important thing to remember is that children need exposure to lessons in all three realms. Lessons are frequently taught in the abstract or semi-concrete. Children need opportunities to have successful experiences that allow them to see, hear and touch the curriculum.

Riding Your Bike for the First Time

Reading books and looking at pictures didn't help when it came to riding a bike. Seeing movies or hearing stories didn't help either. Reading directions or answering questions wouldn't have been of much help. The only thing that teaches anyone the skill of bike riding is bike riding. Doing is learning in almost every skill of life.

GA1339

Powerful
Instructional Techniques

The Importance of Indepth Instruction

A Walk Through the Forest

Have you ever walked through a dense forest? The first time through you break branches and look for some sort of a path. Every time that path is crossed it gets easier and easier until anyone could find his way down the well-worn pathway. If the path is left for many years, the trees overgrow the path, and it once again becomes difficult to find. The path may exist but access to the path is what becomes difficult. This is an analogy to the brain and the process taken on by children when they learn new information. Children need lots of repetition over the path in order to retain the information. Pathways that are raced over and left unattended get lost in the maze of information presented to children.

The Dilemma

As teachers we feel we have so much to teach that we don't have the necessary time. We would like to get more indepth with the content, but we are always pressing on to the next area of the curriculum.

But children need to have a solid base of knowledge that all other information will be built upon. If we build only tiny pathways instead of four-lane highways, what will happen when children go back to retrieve information or build upon their knowledge?

One indictment on American education today is that we are trying to spread ourselves too thin and not developing our curriculum to the extent it needs to be developed for the young mind. We keep passing over material instead of digging down deep.

Solution?

Teachers need to carefully pick and choose what they are going to teach. Second, they need to integrate the curriculum so the important concepts keep appearing in each of the subject areas. Finally, we need to teach with conviction and a belief that every child can and will know the vital pieces of the curriculum.

Learning Is a Social Experience

"Don't talk to your neighbor."
"Put your hands in your lap."
"Please be quiet."
"Children, sit quietly."

Every teacher who has ever walked the earth has probably said those words. Quiet children sitting at their desks with their hands folded, their seats bolted to the floor and sixty children in a classroom was typical in the 1920's as the picture below would indicate. Do individuals learn best when they are isolated from discussion and interaction with other people? We have progressed beyond the belief children need to be seen and not heard, and research has taught us that children do need interaction with other people and their environment in order to learn.

Room 5 St Augustine school Cleveland O

There are lots of different ways that children can work in groups and enjoy interaction such as:

Reading Buddies—Allow children to pair up and read together aloud or silently. Let them take turns reading or asking questions.

Reading Trios—Let one child read, one child record and one child report back the results.

Game Makers—Allow the children to make a classroom game by coloring the game parts, designing some of the rules and teaching other children how to play the game.

Bulletin Board Builders—A group of children may work on the design and development of a class bulletin board.

Math Partners—One child creates the problems and the other solves the problems and then they switch.

Explorers—Groups of children who share an interest in a subject who work together to solve a problem or discover an answer.

Crews—Groups of children who act as the teacher's crew and help with duties from housekeeping to record keeping. The crew can change from week to week.

There are always some drawbacks to allowing children out of their bolted seats, but the benefits outweigh the problems. The first is that allowing children to work in groups requires NOISE. Listen to the type of noise that is being created. Is it creative work noise or silly noise? Children will get off track and not finish. That leads the teacher to a discussion on group responsibility and group cooperation. Building groups that work takes effort and repeated practice, but the payoff is well worth the effort. Cooperative groups of engaged children is an exciting outcome.

GA1339

There is something that is much more scarce, something rarer than ability. It is the ability to recognize ability.

Robert Half

Making Choices

Allowing children to make choices about their environment and their work is one of the strongest motivational tools teachers have available.

The Prison System

In prison the one freedom that is removed is the freedom of choice. The prisoners are still fed, clothed, exercised, do work and see their families. The difference is that they are told what to eat, when to eat, what to wear, who they can see and when they can see them. They have few choices, and they are confined within the system.

Schools aren't prisons but can seem like prisons to children who are constantly forced to conform and never given power over decisions that affect them directly. In a strict environment, principals take on the role of the warden, teachers become the prison guards and the children the inmates.

We don't want schools to become prisons for our children, and yet we also do not want a totally open-ended system where children are given no structure.

42

GA1339

Building on Decision Making Through Choice

Children need opportunities to learn about choices. Limit your selection of items and always think of at least two alternatives when giving an assignment. Here are a few examples of small ways teachers can give children a choice.

- When children are given a page full of math problems, have them choose a selected number to complete. They don't need to do 42 problems when 21 problems will provide the same practice. If given the choice, many children will do the entire page.
- Choose the learning center or learning material you want to use today.
- Choose your partner.
- Choose your seating arrangement.
- As a class, choose the order for the next teaching unit
- Choose to do page 45 or 52 in your math book.

What If Children Make Inappropriate Choices?

The teacher's job is to limit the choices so that only appropriate choices can be made on significant issues. If children persist to make inappropriate choices, then the teacher can step in and take over a particular child's decision as a form of discipline. Children see choices as powerful and part of the gained responsibility of appropriate behavior.

GA1339

Success and Celebration

I never realized this part of teaching existed until I began teaching adults. This is how it came about. In my workshop I incorporated a section where the participants had to unscramble a code that was made up of letters. Some were very difficult and the answers were not easy to identify. I did not allow them to talk to their neighbors or share their answers, and I was rather strict in my demeanor with the group. As soon as they discovered the answers, these adults would throw their hands in the air, bounce in their seats, talk to their neighbors (despite my protests), giggle and smile and laugh. It was like having a room full of second graders. The poor folks who couldn't get the answers got very cross and some expressed later that they felt like walking out of the workshop. This taught me two important lessons as a teacher:

1. Success is a critical factor to learning.
2. When students experience success they celebrate, and when they don't they want to quit.

Celebration

Let's relate that situation to a classroom setting. When children finish papers, their journals, stories or any work, they take a few moments to celebrate. As teachers we worry about this because they will bother their neighbors or get off track or worst of all, they make noise. This is a situation teachers need to work with, anticipate and tolerate.

One strategy is to give children "I'm done" exercises. These are stretches and movements that can be done when the child is done with the work. Another solution is to let the child acknowledge his completed work some place in the classroom by checking off his name, putting up a star or crossing off his number. (Crossing off an item on a list is particularly satisfying for visual people who get a sense of completion from a list that is crossed off.)

Recognize the need to celebrate, and then watch it happen in every walk of life. Everywhere you go you will see people doing little acts of celebration at the conclusion of their work.

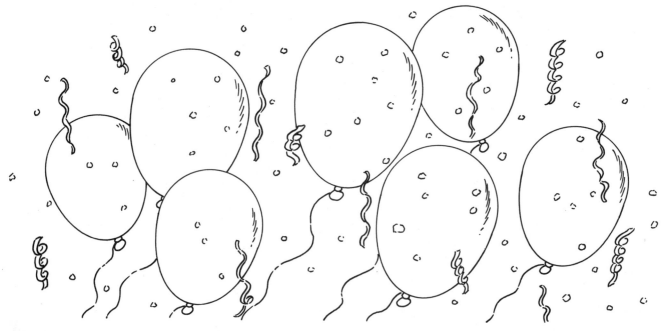

GA1339

Success and Struggle

Knowing the boundaries between challenge, struggle and the rewards of success is a difficult determination for a new teacher. The American work ethic suggested struggle and challenge as part of our heritage. The motto is "no pain, no gain." This is true in some situations, but it is equally true that very few people persist in unsuccessful situations.

Do you have a project that you started and then abandoned? We usually abandon these projects because they have met with some measure of failure. Where do these abandoned projects rest in our homes? Craft projects in closets, woodworking in the garage, somewhere that doesn't remind us that we gave up! What happens to children who have unsuccessful school experiences? Where do they put their feelings about their lack of ability? Do they hide it behind poor behavior, lack of attention or just push it away with the hope that it will never be noticed?

What will it take to get your project out of mothballs and begin to work on it again? Will another failure throw it back into mothballs? Will further failure and persistent challenge force that child to move forward? Would struggle motivate you as an adult?

It is human nature to be drawn toward success. It is powerful, positive and engaging. Adults are large, overgrown versions of children, and success works for both groups equally. Building success into instruction is difficult but not impossible. Much of "success teaching" has to do with the quality of instruction on the part of the teacher and the sensitivity to the needs and abilities of the children.

GA1339

Teaching Is Risky Business and If It Isn't, It Ought to Be

I personally love to play my piano, even though I don't play very well. When I practice I follow the notes carefully and the song sounds just fine, not great, not exciting, but fine. I want to play my songs with passion, but if I do that, I will risk making a mistake. I hate making mistakes! But if I take the risk and play with passion, the songs sound so much better—they flow and there is excitement in the music. I do make some mistakes, but the risk is worth the flubs. I feel as if I have given it my best; I've risked failure and met up with success.

Teach with joy, passion and a level of risk. If your light bulb is on low wattage, your classroom will be dim.

What kind of risks am I talking about? Well, try the new approach for reading or math. Do the silly song with the children and dance along. Take on the science fair even if you have no idea what you are doing. Try making home visits this year. Try writing a grant for a project you have always wanted to try. Start a Friday Lunch Bunch with your faculty and have a potluck lunch with your fellow teachers one or two Fridays a month. In other words, *step out from the ordinary into the extraordinary.*

I want every teacher's tombstone to read, "He/She lived the ordinary life in an extraordinary way."

Go for It!

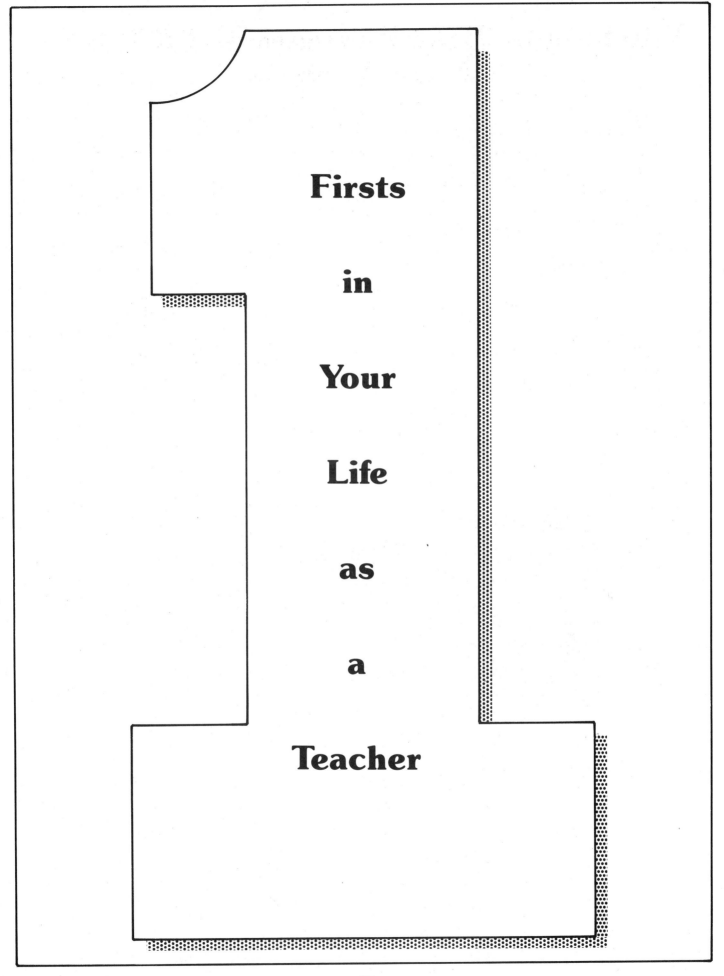

Firsts

in

Your

Life

as

a

Teacher

GA1339

First Fire Drills and Other States of Emergency

A Word from the Wise

Carol Breen
Principal
Grand Haven, Michigan

During my first few weeks as a new teacher, I practiced the fire and tornado procedures with my classroom children. I was very proud of their progress, and I was ready for the news of our first drill. I was informed that we would have our drill at 10:30 in the morning. I was confident! When the alarm rang I had my children take the emergency tornado posture on the interior wall that had been designated. I had my class roster, my flashlight and was down on the floor with my very quiet children. Suddenly the door opened and the principal was staring at us with shock and surprise. "Mrs. Breen, the bell you heard was the FIRE alarm." My advice to all teachers is "know your bells!"

Fire drills and other safety precautions need to be taken very seriously by the teacher. Anything can happen and children can be seriously hurt if precautions are not taken. Here are a few tips to remember.

- Keep a copy of your class list, a flashlight and any other important document or necessary tool in a stringed bag very near the door of the classroom. Grab it as you exit the door.
- A class list is an important piece of information. In a real emergency you want to make sure you have every child. Check the class list or daily attendance list as a practice at each drill.
- Many children go to special classes and flow from classroom to classroom. Keep a special list that reminds you of who is where, when.
- During drills remember to remind children that this is a practice and that a fire is not happening in the building. Young children can become very fearful and panic during a drill.
- Insist on quiet and good behavior. This is a time for the strictest of behavior expectation. A life could depend on quiet, quick behavior.
- Make sure you know the correct exit or emergency procedure for each classroom you visit with your children. That means the library, gym or cafeteria.

RIVERSIDE SCHOOL

GA1339

First Open House

Open House is that night of nights when the lights shine, decorations go up and the parents enter. Some open houses include parents and children, some have a presentation and brief classroom visit, other schools restrict the evening to parents. Whatever the organization system, the school's goal is to introduce the parents to their child's teacher, classroom and school; and the parents' objective is to find out how their child is adjusting to the school setting and getting a glimpse of the child's day in school.

Teachers feel an obligation to speak with each parent for a few moments and welcome them to the classroom. The most often-asked question by the parent will be, "How is _____ doing?" It is asked as both a question of interest and concern, but sometimes it leads to discussions that need to be held in private. Encourage parents to set up conferences if needed and make your comments about the children positive during open house.

Open House Ideas

- Trace the children's bodies and have them color in the clothing. The bodies can be taped into the children's seats with stories about school on their desks. The teacher can tape them to the wall outside the class with their arms pointing to the room.
- Videotape the children in the classroom, on the playground, at lunch, in the gym and library. Let the children narrate the video, and encourage them to share the special parts of their school. This can be shown on the TV monitor during open house.
- Have an open house treasure hunt where parents or parents and children have to answer questions about details in the room and the building. Make the hunt short but fun and informative. Often parents pass by interesting classroom materials because they don't realize their purpose.
- Ask the parents to leave story starters for the children's lesson the next day. These are briefly described situations that engage the children into continuing the story.
- Try to be sensitive to the children whose parents do not attend open house. One solution is to encourage the parents to come in with the child at their convenience to visit the classroom or make some time before or after conferences for a classroom visit.

GA1339

First Sick Child

A Word from the Wise

Linda Kochan
Physical Education Teacher
Nordonia City Schools
Nordonia, Ohio

One of the most exciting activities in my class is the parachute. The little children always get so excited and some get totally carried away. This has led to throwing up on the parachute and wet pants. One week I washed the parachute three times. My word to teachers is be flexible and remove the other children so you don't end up with a secondary reaction. Deal with the child who has had the problem with compassion and understanding.

Dealing with an accident of a sick child can be a real crazy maker for any teacher, new or veteran. I had a child who vomited every day for the first six weeks of kindergarten, and it was always unexpected. It can be difficult. Here are some guidelines.

1. Don't panic—stay calm and concentrate on the child who is in trouble and get the green stuff!

2. Separate the other children and get them busy on a task.

3. If it is serious, get help as fast as possible.

4. If the child loses consciousness or seems to have a broken bone, keep the child stationary unless the child is in danger.

5. Try to make the child feel as comfortable as possible.

6. Remember that with the new regulations around the issue of AIDS, it is necessary to follow your school directions for cleanup. Children should never be involved in the cleanup.

7. Make sure that the other children in the class deal with the sick child compassionately. Discuss openly with the class the need for kind and considerate treatment when someone has a problem.

GA1339

First Field Trip

Field trips are one of the most beneficial school activities for children. A good field trip should have the following elements:

The field trip should be educationally beneficial. Make sure that your field trip destination is a place where the children can learn new concepts. That means that the site and concepts should not be above their ability. If a presentation is made, it should match the ability level and interest of the students. This is often hard to control, but teachers should keep in close contact with the field trip site and make sure the age and needs of the children are communicated.

Lessons should lead into the trip. Teaching a unit prior to a field trip can be great fun for children and heighten the educational benefits of the trip. As a teacher it is helpful to visit the site prior to the trip to gather information for the lessons.

Plan early. The good sites for field trips get booked early and teachers need to plan ahead. Try to remember every element by walking through the day. For example, a trip to the zoo would include this type of planning:

1. Helpers would arrive early to help with grouping of children and name tags.

2. Children will have their own lunches, and they will need to be collected.

3. Children will be carrying money for drinks and treats—remember to limit the amount they can carry.

4. Double check with the bus the day before departure or have a parent call each driver to remind him/her of the day and time.

5. Double check the list for permission slips and send them to the office the morning of the field trip with the attendance list.

GA1339

6. Keep a list of the groups' and parents' first and last names with phone numbers of the school and children's numbers. Take this list along on the field trip.

7. Discuss proper behavior with your children and let them know the consequences for poor behavior on the bus or at the field trip site itself. If you have some children who are extremely difficult, you may want to (or have to) keep them close at hand. If you have difficulty with a student in a confined classroom, imagine the trouble a volunteer parent could have on a field trip.

8. If possible, have the parent helpers travel in two's with larger groups of children. If there should be an accident, then one parent can deal with the emergency and the other can continue on with the group.

9. Talk to the bus driver about directions and make sure he/she is familiar with the correct route. Don't assume drivers know where they are going or the best route. Teachers should have maps available.

10. Parents and children should both have name tags. Parents can just have their names so they can speak freely with each other, and children should have their names and the name, address and phone number of the school on the tags.

11. I personally feel that if at all possible, teachers should not have their own group of children on field trips but should move from group to group throughout the day. This allows the teacher time to get the group through the front gate, get the lunch area arranged and prepare for the departure. It also keeps the teacher free in case of an emergency and each group of children enjoys the company of the teacher throughout the day.

12. Lunch during the day can be handled a variety of ways. The easiest is to have each group eat independently of the next, and have the parent helpers carry the lunches. Sometimes the lunches need to be cooled and carried to a site for a group lunch. If this is the case, make sure that help is available for carrying the heavy coolers and boxes of lunches.

13. Make sure everyone is very clear as to the time and exact spot for the departure. Many school buses need to leave early to take children home and cannot afford to be late. The children also may need to be back in time for their own buses.

14. Count heads; count heads; count heads!

Education Follow-up. The true educational benefit can come as the teacher follows up the field trip with extension activities and discussion about the visit. The visit may also bring about other questions and lead to extended activities.

Here are some field trip follow-up suggestions:

- Make a large wall mural explaining the field trip.
- Make a class video of the field trip.
- Make classroom books that tell about the activity.
- Have the children tell about their trip to a class of younger children.
- Prepare a food that was seen on the field trip.
- Have someone from the field trip visit the school so the children can share their environment.
- Write thank-you notes to the people at the field trip site or volunteer helpers.
- Ask the children to draw parts of the field trip and put them together in a diorama.
- Read stories that continue the field trip theme. A funny book about a field trip is *The Day Jimmy's Boa Ate the Wash* by Trinka Hakes Noble, pictures by Steven Kellogg.

First Formal Observation

Being observed as a new classroom teacher is upsetting to some teachers and of little significance to others. Here are some dos and don'ts for your first observation.

Do—Plan the lesson with careful attention to objectives that match the procedures.

Don't—Try a lesson that is meant to be "showy." If possible, stay with the familiar and demonstrate the students' developed abilities.

Do—Stay calm, relaxed and don't lose your sense of humor.

Don't—Stay up half the night preparing and come to school tired and lackluster.

Do—Integrate the lesson with other subject areas and attempt to draw in themes from other curriculum areas such as making mention of a math story problem as part of a social studies lesson.

Don't—Get flustered if students misbehave. Stay relaxed and calmly deal with the problem.

Do—Keep your eyes on your students. Don't make eye contact with the observer. Focus on the children.

Do—Allow for interaction in the lesson. The observer should be able to witness the teacher interacting with the students and students interacting with the classroom materials and other students.

Do—Prepare a lesson in writing that is given to the observer. Include the objectives, procedures, materials and expected outcomes.

Do—Have a place for the observer to sit and a place for his/her coat if necessary.

Do—Ask to see your written observation report if a meeting is not scheduled by the administration.

Don't—Be surprised if the person observing has little expertise in your subject area. Take the time to share your reasoning for the lesson development if you feel the observer may not clearly see your motivation.

Do—Use this as an opportunity to demonstrate the good judgement they used when deciding to hire you!

GA1339

A Word from the Wise

Mary Voigt is the Secondary Language Arts Supervisor for Pearland Independent School District in Pearland, Texas. In the past, Mary has worked with elementary teachers in reading and language arts.

Teachers new to Texas teaching need some solace or advice concerning the Texas Teacher Appraisal System. Usually that promotes a great deal of anxiety. Here are tidbits for dealing with teacher appraisal.

1. Avoid discussions about your anxiety or others' anxiety. This only increases the anxiety.

2. Believe in yourself.

3. Refuse to listen to "horror" stories.

4. Teach as if no one were in the room observing you; center your attention on the children.

5. Don't share results with anyone. If you score higher you will be resented and if you don't you will feel inferior. (Teachers have told me this one!)

6. Remember that there are no perfect human beings, and areas that need improvement are not shameful.

7. Try to keep your lesson as routine and normal as you can; that will keep the children from becoming nervous.

8. Learn from your mistakes.

9. Remember that many indicators overlap and one action often covers behaviors. In other words, don't be overwhelmed with the sheer number of indicators.

First Party

There are different kinds of classroom parties. Some parties are holiday celebrations while others are used as rewards for a job well done. Some parties can be well-planned and involved while others can be spur-of-the-moment celebrations. Children love celebrations. The excitement and anticipation can work for or against a teacher. Here are some guidelines for party planning.

1. Check out the school policy on having parties before you begin. Some schools don't sanction parties for certain holidays, and you may find your school has a school celebration rather than individual classroom parties.
2. Find out the school's tradition on who, what and when for parties. Being in touch with the school culture on this issue is very important. Teachers may say, "We always have a Halloween parade." Traditions exist in families and schools and some time honored practices need to be acknowledged.
3. Reward parties for long-term good behavior or a major project well done can be very motivational to children. The best thing to do is to get the children themselves busy planning and preparing the party. When children are involved in the planning, they take more enjoyment from the activity.
4. If parents are planning a party for the children, make sure you keep in close contact to see that the time line and the activities fit the children. Make sure that the party is realistic, not too simple yet also not too complex. Older students enjoy being part of a party planning committee.
5. Make sure that everyone realizes that cleanup is part of the party. Children can leave quite a mess and the classroom teacher should not be left to finish the party cleanup.
6. If parents are organizing the party, it is best to stay with your children throughout the party. The parents are not legally responsible for any problem that might occur, and they may not be able to keep control of a classroom of children. Parties should also be shared enjoyment for teachers and children.
7. Finally, don't let the parties get out of hand. The activities should be fun and of interest to children. Don't worry about fancy decorations. Spend the energy on the games and activities that the children enjoy the most.

56

First Parent-Teacher Conference

Having been both a parent and a teacher at parent-teacher conferences, I can honestly say that I would rather play the role of teacher to parent. As a parent, you walk into a room to talk about somone you love with all your heart and soul. You know your child's problems but love him/her for his/her strengths and weaknesses. As the teacher begins to share your child's areas of need, no matter how kindly, you feel upset. It is not rational, but it is a fact that most parents have a difficult time hearing negative remarks about their children. As a teacher, it is very important to realize that you are talking to someone who unconditionally loves this child. You may personally find the child quite difficult, but remember that the parent sees the sun rise and set on that child's face!

1. Start the conference on a positive note. The most effective starter is to tell the parent a personal, positive anecdote about his/her child. Jot down notes about a witnessed act of kindness or a particular interest of the child. You might even mention a particular job well done or anything that says to the parent that you KNOW his/her child and recognize his/her specialness.

2. When sharing areas of needed improvement, give concrete examples. Instead of talking about immature behavior, relate the incident when the child used poor judgement by sticking out his foot to trip another child. Parents can relate to incidents but can not relate to catchy phrases.

3. Give the parent a starting and ending time for the conference. Make the time long enough, if possible, to allow some conversation with the parent. Ask the parent to share his/her child's attitudes about school and his/her classmates.

4. Don't let conversations wander off to siblings and other topics. Often parents will compare their children during the conference, or the topic may drift off the child. Make sure that the conference is about the child and not personal issues unrelated to the child.

GA1339

5. If you have a laundry list of problems and complaints about the child, try to limit the list to a few major problems. Parents need to feel that there is something they can affect and will be overwhelmed by too many problems. A conference is also an information-gathering time for the teacher. Listen to the parent and learn about some new facets of the student.

6. Give the parents concrete, viable, available ideas for helping their child with the problems. Suggest ideas that will be workable and remember that this child may be one of five children who each has his/her own needs. If both parents work or the child is from a one-parent household, remember that additional time at home with the child on the part of the parent may not be a viable solution.

7. Use the Parent-Teacher Conference form at the conclusion of the conference to remind you of any important conversation from those who attended the conference.

8. Remember to listen as well as talk. Conferences give teachers insight into the lives of the children they teach.

9. End the conference on a positive note. Smile and be genuine and sincere when you say farewell.

10. Keep a brief log of conferences. This will allow you to review what was said or remember what was covered at a previous conference. This type of action will keep you, the teacher, accountable.

GA1339

Parent-Teacher Conferences

Teacher: _____

Date _____

Parents _____ **Student** _____

Comments _____

_____

_____

_____

_____

Teacher: _____

Date _____

Parents _____ **Student** _____

Comments _____

_____

_____

_____

_____

Teacher: _____

Date _____

Parents _____ **Student** _____

Comments _____

_____

_____

_____

GA1339

First Upset Parent

When a parent becomes upset about a school issue, it can quickly become emotionally charged. The first and most important rule is to listen carefully and try to determine the problem. The problem may be unrelated to the issue at hand, so try to listen to hear the true problem. When children get into trouble, the parents may take ownership for the problem and the parents' ego may be at stake. Understand that the parents may be expressing their own frustration over the situation and that it may stem from a family problem that is outside the immediate view of the teacher. Teachers often have to act as counselors and may end up working with families to solve their problems.

If you feel that the issue is too difficult or that the parent is upset with you, then seek outside help from your administration or another teacher. Don't be afraid to ask for help. No teacher is capable of handling every situation.

Parents do not have the right to call you at home on a consistent basis to discuss their child's needs and problems. Occasionally you will find a parent who will repeatedly call on the telephone, and it is important to clearly state that you prefer a face-to-face conference and set a date and time.

If the conference with the parent does become "charged," notify the principal and record any comments and remarks. Share these with your principal as soon as possible.

GA1339

The Real Nitty-Gritty of Teaching

GA1339

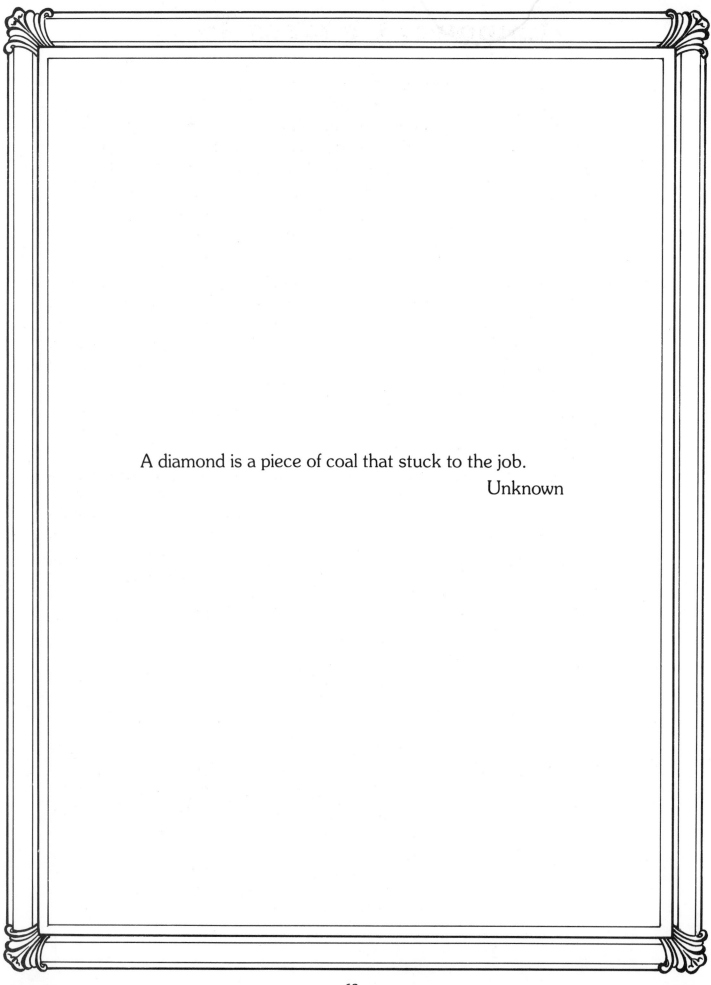

A diamond is a piece of coal that stuck to the job.

Unknown

Empower Children To. . .

Organize
Resolve Conflict
Take the Initiative
Use Their Imagination
Sense Ownership
Create the Rules
Make Decisions

Have you ever watched a group of children play with toys that are modeled after a television cartoon? They try to make the toy do everything that it does in the cartoon. The play is identical to the TV show and the children show no open-ended thinking.

How about a baseball game for little folks. The adults coach, run the game and tell the children what to do, step by step. Children don't go out and pick up a neighborhood game because they only play when it's scheduled by adults.

Have you ever seen children on a playground who run to the monitor every other moment with a complaint about another child? They don't know how to start a game on the playground without the help of an adult leader.

These same children find themselves in classrooms with teachers (adults), who are trying to hold everything in complete order, every moment. The adult monitors the learning stations, makes the rules, acts as judge and jury when it comes to altercations and basically runs the show.

One of the first steps for every healthy adult is a step toward independence. Independence is not something that is thrust on you at eighteen years of age. Independence is built every day and every week by people around the child. We help children learn the steps to independence by empowering them to BELIEVE IN THEIR ABILITIES.

Empower Children To. . .

Organize
Resolve Conflict
Take the Initiative
Use Their Imagination
Sense Ownership
Create the Rules
Make Decisions

Giving Directions

Teachers give hundreds of directions to children every day. The directions range from simple statements about getting in line to very complex directions concerning the completion of work. A classroom exchange can sound something like this:

"I want everyone to listen as we get ready to do these papers. Is everyone listening? I want everyone to complete the following three pages for reading. Joey, would you mind closing the door? We have some noise in the hall. Sarah, would you get my chalk liner off my desk? OK, on the first page I would like you to read the short story and then quietly retell the story to your reading buddy. Together I want you to write a short paragraph about how you think this story should end. Discuss this with your partner and put both of your names on the paper. On the second sheet I want you to list the spelling words from the story. See how many you can find and then write the sentence where they are found in the story. On the last sheet I would like you to draw a picture of one of the characters from the story and write his/her name and what he/she did in the story. When you are done with the three pages, put your buddy reader paper in the basket and your own work in your file and check off your name so I know it has been handed in. Any questions?"

All in all that comes to twenty different directions for the children to listen to and filter through, some not directed at them but all floating in their direction. This type of dialogue is very typical, and it is amazing that most children do as well as they do when it comes to following directions.

It is a national fact that the most asked question in school is "What are we supposed to do?" This question is usually whispered in the ear of the neighboring child.

As teachers we need to be sensitive to the fact that the room is filled with a variety of different learning styles, and many children cannot absorb a complex set of directions. In fact most adults can also not absorb a complex set of directions.

One way to help children follow directions and yet give them responsibility is to outline the steps in both the auditory and visual. Write the steps on the chalkboard and tell the steps that need to be completed. This also helps children's reading skills. Teachers of young children can give directions using rebus pictures for nonreaders.

Listen to yourself carefully and look into the eyes of the children to see if they are following your directions. Check their work and don't assume it is their inability when the work comes back incomplete. Always try to be a reflective teacher.

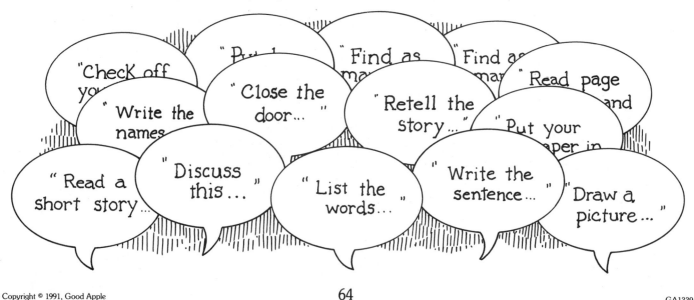

GA1339

Discipline

A Word from the Wise

Joan Aldrich Knight
Callaghan Memorial
Kindergarten/Chapter I
Vermont

During my first years as a teacher I moved from Vermont to a town in the south. It was there that I learned about corporal punishment. I survived until about February without resorting to this method. One day I had finally had it with one of my third-grade boys, and I took him to the office for a "paddling." He leaned over the principal's desk—I drew back the paddle . . . . . closed my eyes . . . . and with a loud whack . . . hit the desk! We were both so startled and relieved. We went back to the classroom with no one the wiser, except me. I've never used corporal punishment since.

Discipline is one of the most complicated and yet simple tasks of a teacher. There are no easy answers or absolute solutions since each situation and each child is quite different. There are some realizations that need to come along with each teacher as he/she begins to discipline children.

1. Teachers need to be consistent with their requirements for behavior.

2. The rules need to be simple and kept to a reasonable number.

3. Children need to clearly understand the expectations.

4. Children have to learn to accept the responsibility for their behavior and accept the consequences for their actions.

5. Teachers must stay calm and not yell or lose control. When you lose control you are now the proud owner of the problem. The child will transfer the problem on to the teacher. "She is upset that I got in a fight" rather than "I got into a fight."

6. Discipline needs to fit the offense and quickly follow the offense in terms of time.

7. Children need to know that they are still liked and cared for despite the altercation.

Homework

Every school and school district has their own policy on homework. Some districts feel that mandatory homework is an important element in student achievement while other districts may discourage excessive homework. The teacher's first responsibility is to get a feeling for district and building homework expectations.

Make sure that the homework is always a review or extension of a concept previously taught in school. Children and parents can spend some frustrating evenings hammering over concepts that are totally new to the child. Homework can be work that was not completed in school, work that is directed toward a project or an extension on a unit or lesson.

Many times teachers develop units in their classroom and develop a project that is complete at home and may need a great deal of attention from parents. Make sure that the project is within the time and money constraints that are typical to your community. Don't make the participation difficult for children who may receive little or no family support. At the same time don't be afraid to get the children involved because of a few who will not be able to participate.

If you start a homework schedule, stick to it. Let the children know that on Monday they should do reading, Tuesday is for math homework and spelling practice. Wednesday is the day to work on social studies and science, and Thursday night is the review for spelling and math. These types of predictable schedules help the children and parents keep the homework schedule and give everyone a clear view of expectations.

If a test is scheduled and the children study and are prepared, do everything within your power to administer the test on the designated day. Children who have studied and parents who have helped them prepare for the exam will be frustrated with delays.

Younger children need a homework reminder that can be sent home daily or weekly, and older children can keep homework notebooks with their assignments. Some children will never remember their homework, and if they remember to do it, they will forget to return the homework to school.

Homework Raffle

Have the homework monitor hand out a raffle ticket to each child who has returned his homework each day. A supply of raffle tickets can be purchased, duplicated or you can duplicate the ones on the following page. Each returned homework paper gives the child a chance at the Friday afternoon raffle. The prizes can be passes to a day of no homework or an ice-cream ticket for lunch. Children respond very well to these types of activities.

GA1339

Raffle Tickets

Name:		Name:		Name:		Name:
Date:		Date:		Date:		Date:

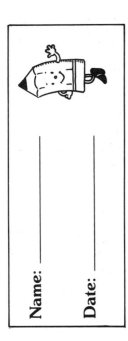

Homework

Week of	
Monday	
Tuesday	
Wednesday	
Thursday	
Don't Forget	

GA1339

Hand Raising

The tradition of every school in America is to have students raise their hands when they are ready to give responses. It makes such sense. Everyone can't talk at one time, and everyone needs to take a turn. The teacher asks a question and a group of children raise their hands with an answer. Keep close attention to who raises their hands. Does everyone raise their hands, or do the same children repeatedly raise their hands?

When "Mary Sunshine" raises her hand, "Joe Buzzard" can stop thinking because he is sure that Mary has the answer, and it is probably a correct answer. Why bother when it's easier to let her go for the glory. What happens when a teacher asks a question and calls on any student without the hands being raised? Suddenly everyone has to think because they have an equal chance to be called on for an answer. Make sure that when hands are raised the other children don't shut down. Providing a wait time between the time a question is asked and the time for raised hands may also keep everyone thinking and learning.

Clean Desks

It can be a terrifying experience to look into some children's desks. It is particularly upsetting when you see something move! Some children have organization skills of a pack rat and some desks look like those potential executive secretaries.

For most children there is very little motivation to clean their desks. Try a visit by the desk fairy. Children never know when the desk fairy may visit, and she always leaves a little fairy dust (glitter) and a treat (small candy works well). The children with the cleanest or most improved desks are sure to try a bit harder.

As the children get older, try to motivate organizational skills with class passes for a baseball game or a popcorn party. Everyone has to be caught with a clean desk during the month. If everyone gets a clean pass, the group gets a party. The pressure from peers to try really is effective. This can also be done with homework.

GA1339

Grades, Grades and More Grades

GA1339

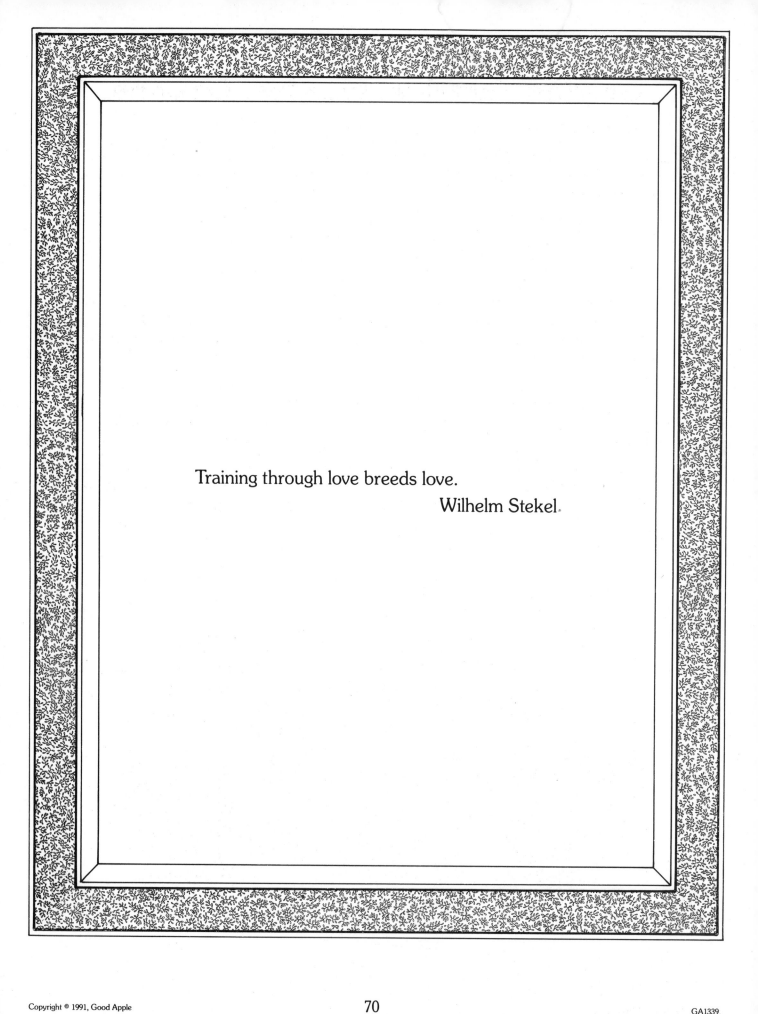

Training through love breeds love.

Wilhelm Stekel.

70

GA1339

Grades, Grades, Grades, Grades

1. Know the school policy on grading for your particular grade level.

2. Develop a consistent system for grading. Let children know that different things have different weights such as homework and classroom may be graded differently than quizzes and tests.

3. Make sure your marks have meaning to the children. If you write the number correct at the top of the paper, will the child know what needs to be corrected? One of the best systems is to write the number incorrect out of the possible number correct for each paper. This gives the child a comparison.

4. Don't overgrade a paper with red X's, circles and lines. Children will not learn from the errors but just feel overwhelmed by the mistakes. Pick out one problem such as spelling errors on poor papers and address those areas or put a message on the paper that the child should see you for a visit.

5. When a child fails a test, give the child an opportunity to take the test over and average the grades. Our objective is to have children learn, and a second chance at the test gives one more opportunity for learning. Retaking the test also sends the child the message that this is important and needs to be learned!

6. Sometimes we let children grade each other's papers and they erase the answers. After completing a paper, the children can lightly cover their work with yellow crayon. Once the pencil has been covered with the wax, it is impossible to erase.

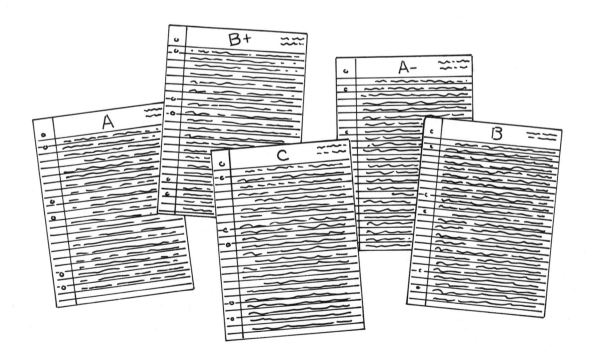

GA1339

7. Letting children grade their own papers can be a helpful experience. After the papers have been graded, let the children meet in groups according to the questions missed. See if together they can arrive at an answer to some of the difficult problems.

8. Don't use sad faces for grading papers. There is nothing sad about making a mistake—it's all part of life.

9. Use a variety of colors when grading papers—they keep children's attention.

10. Every child likes something on his paper that acknowledges that you took the time to overview his work. Stamp pads, stamps or real stamps from inexpensive stamp-collecting kits work also.

11. Intermediate children starting around fourth grade seem to enter into a self-imposed grade consciousness. They may ask what the numbers mean or ask for letter grades. It is at this stage that children begin to compare themselves with their peers, and they want to know how they are doing.

12. When you give a writing assignment, make sure to take the time to make comments. Comments on writing can be reaction or evaluative. For most casual classroom writing in journals, the work should be reacted to and not evaluated. But written work for reports should be evaluated.

GA1339

Tacit Knowledge

Jerry is the kind of kid who can fix anything. Put a tool in his hand and he will have the gadget apart in minutes, and what's more amazing, he can put it back together. Jerry has a hard time in school; he can't sit still, and he hates all the paperwork.

Becky is a quiet, average student. She was so quiet it was easy to pass her by until we got the new student from Korea. Our new student didn't speak a word of English and was truly afraid of school. Becky came forward without being asked and helped our new student with a calm understanding and sensitivity.

David is a very athletic child who loves to play any type of sports. All of his school stories relate to sports and any kind of athletic competition. David wants to grow up to play baseball. That is a very strong dream for David.

Mary Jane is wonderful at keeping me on track. She remembers the assembly that I nearly forgot, and she always notices where I leave the staple gun and my scissors. She is quick to put jobs in order and works in a very systematic approach to her school studies.

Each of these students displays various forms of tacit knowledge. Tacit knowledge is related to a person's ability to deal with everyday living. None of these students were exceptional academic students, but in each case they showed an area of talent for life skills.

As a teacher you may find children such as Jerry who can learn about something just by looking at it or by watching someone else complete a task. Or you may have a David in your class who has strong kinesthetic skills. Mary Jane can quickly organize and prioritize in any given situation, and Becky displays compassion and an ability to get along with many different types of people.

As these children grow they may surprise the teacher. Jerry just might grow up to be a surgeon, and Mary Jane may be running her own company. Although schools don't acknowledge the skills that truly relate to life, they are essential to our development. Oh yes, I didn't forget David and Becky. Their teacher looked at them one day and said, "You're good enough to be teachers," and that's just what they grew up to be, great teachers!

GA1339

I'm a Good Person Even If I Don't Get Good Grades

School is a society that is totally consumed with academic achievement. Whether it be preschool, elementary, high school or college, the grade reigns supreme. But if grades are so important, why is it that political candidates don't post their report cards as part of their campaigns? Did our United States President flunk civics? We'll never know. In truth, the "real" world seldom looks at academic achievement but instead looks at the individual's ability to communicate, think creatively, work effectively or contribute to society.

In high school most of us knew who was "smart." Many of those students were held in high esteem because they were able to do well on tests and give the teacher the required responses. In the "real" world these people may or may not have found personal success. Success in life is a much more complicated issue.

When we hand students their grades on their report cards, it is important to instill in them the feeling that these grades reflect only one small portion of their ability. If they did well, then it means that they are good at schoolwork, but many children are good at other things that don't show on report cards. Share with the children some of the talents you have seen in your room that are not expressed on the report cards, such as friendship, loyalty, patience, perserverance, kindness and generosity. Let the children know that you like them and care about each of them equally no matter what kind of grades they received.

Finally, children need to be encouraged to work toward improving their grades because they want to improve their grades for themselves. They are not in competition with each other; they are in a competition with themselves. Neither the teacher nor the parent own those grades; those grades belong to each student, no matter what age. They are theirs to take pride in and to improve. As teachers and parents, when we take the praise or the blame for students' grades, we take with us the motivation and ownership that rightfully belongs to each child.

GA1339

Accountability

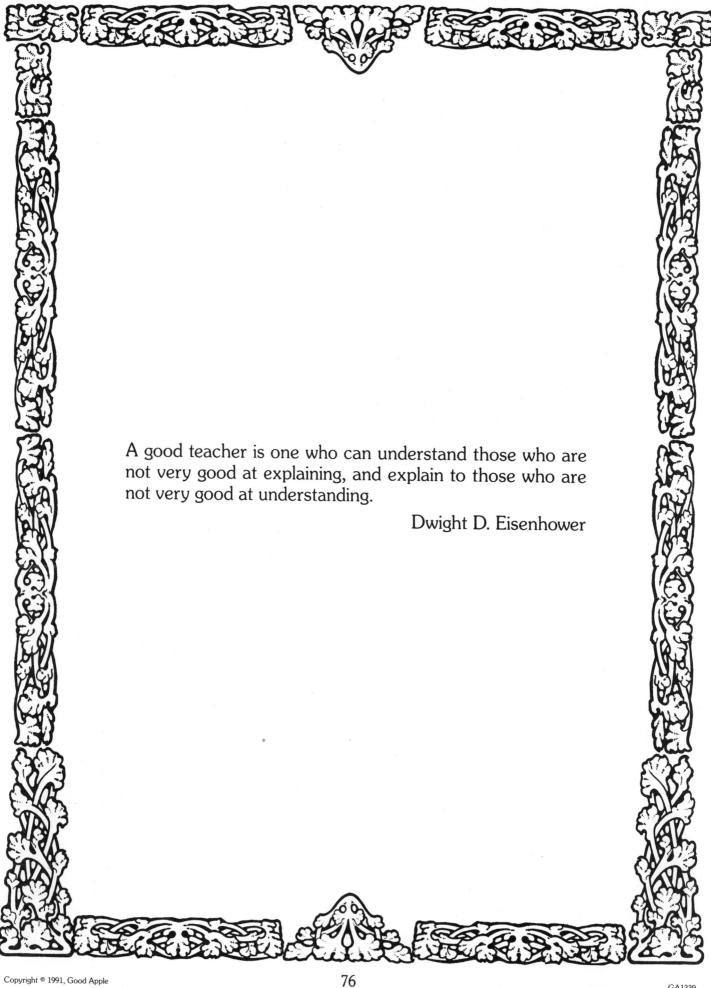

A good teacher is one who can understand those who are not very good at explaining, and explain to those who are not very good at understanding.

Dwight D. Eisenhower

Being a Diagnostician

After I had taught for a number of years, I found myself in line at a grocery store observing all the children standing with their parents and sitting in the carts. I would look at the gate of one child as she walked and was concerned because the right foot turned in too far. Another child had some speech problems that would require speech therapy. Another child was very hyper and tense, and the parent did not seem to notice the child's erratic movements and disruption. I realized that as a teacher I always look at children differently. I study them and watch their movements. I listen to their words and how those words fit their meanings. I study their eyes to see if they dart or are steady and sure. Being a teacher is being a student of human behavior.

You may enjoy the sport of people watching, and child watching is a similar activity that will make you a better teacher every day. If you carefully observe children you will note behaviors that are consistent across the particular age. Your children may all have trouble sharing, or they may constantly be tattling on each other. Look for the underlying reasons for the behavior. Try to determine what has caused the trend.

Watch your children at lunch, on the playground and in life. Listen not only to what they say but also how they say it. Many times learning problems have very little to do with learning. Try to determine what is at the heart and soul of each child.

When you have a child who is having a difficult social problem or learning problem, start with some observation time. Look for unusual behavior or subtle difference in the way the child responds. This is like being a detective, and you as the teacher play the part of Sherlock Holmes. If the problem is difficult, don't be afraid to call in Dr. Watson, your principal or support staff.

Being good at identifying a problem is being good at knowing about people and their needs and perceptions. Every teacher needs to build these skills in order to identify and service the needs of the children they teach.

GA1339

How Do We Measure Success in Children?

One of the personally rewarding activities is to keep a comprehensive portfolio of each child's work. This is good for evaluation of the child and helps the teacher see the process. Think of it as a scrapbook so keep artwork, random photographs of projects, a tape recording of the child reading, journal entries, stories or anything that is reflective of the child. Everyone doesn't need to have the same things in his file. Make it a mixture so it reflects the individual child. And instead of your trying to keep up with the filing, let the children suggest additions and add to the files themselves.

At the conclusion of the year sit down personally with each child and talk over the file. Discuss what progress you have seen as a teacher. Talk about your goals as a teacher and how they were met by the child. Discuss areas that still need work. This should be a positive, enhancing experience for both you and the child. It should be, in some respects, a sentimental journey.

GA1339

How Do We Measure Our Success as Teachers?

Where do I stand as a teacher? In the "real world" if you are doing a good job, you get raises and promotions. In teaching, your salary will seldom reflect your effort. Was I successful with my students? In the real world you'll have increased sales, higher profits or better products. In teaching you have test scores and grades that don't always reflect a true picture of your ability as a teacher. It's so hard to measure your success.

Many teachers compare themselves to their peers. Since we usually don't watch each other actually teach, we use other gauges of success such as pretty bulletin boards, quiet children or nice artwork. These are the kinds of things you can see when you walk down a hall or peek in a classroom. Those things don't identify good teaching. Most indicators we use don't help us detect how we are doing in comparison to another teacher.

I was considered to be a good teacher, but in all my years of teaching, I felt I had one really good year. At the conclusion of most years I felt that I hadn't really reached some children, that I hadn't achieved what I had wanted with others and that I wished I could do a better job overall. That is the one element of teaching that is most difficult—you can never be done. There is always a way to make the product better and do a better job. Even great test scores don't reflect the child who never socialized or the child who produced despite difficult behavior.

No teacher can reach or teach all children. Children grow like flowers. It's difficult to see the process and some buds may not bloom under our care. It may take another teacher another year to bring the flower to full bloom.

Because we often teach in isolation, we have unrealistic scales for measuring our success.

GA1339

You and Your Students

GA1339

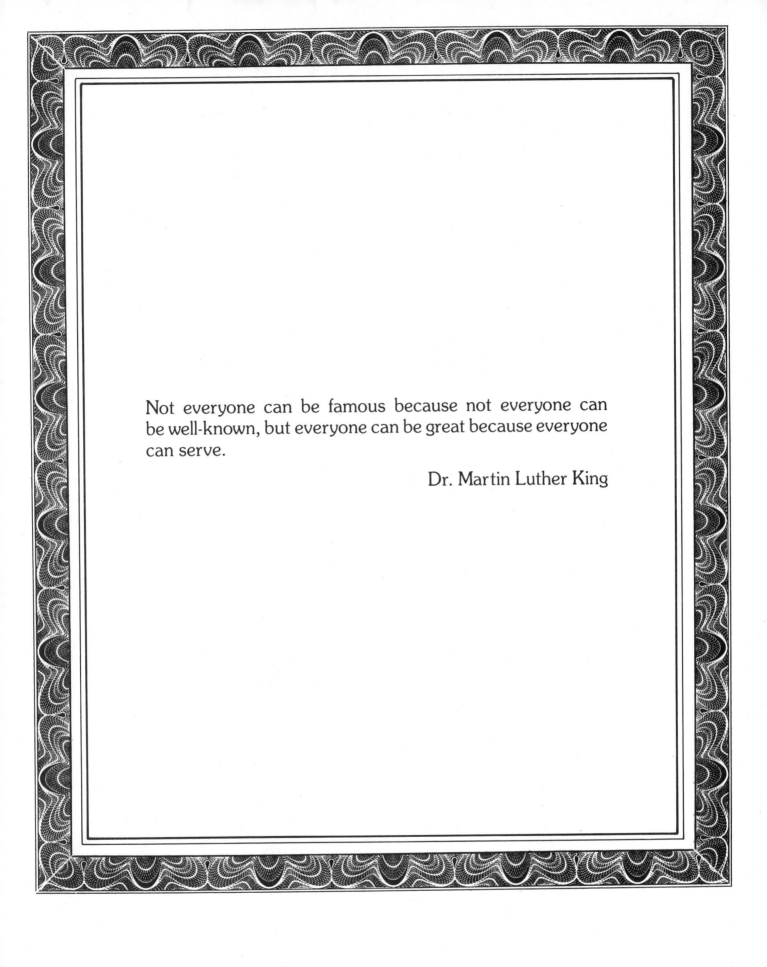

Not everyone can be famous because not everyone can be well-known, but everyone can be great because everyone can serve.

Dr. Martin Luther King

81

GA1339

The Issue of Respect

The rules are simple—respect yourself, respect others and respect the environment. For young and older children those simple rules clearly say what we expect in our schools, in our classrooms and in the world. Young children may not understand the issue of respect, but the word should be taught starting as soon as possible.

One of the biggest issues facing America today is the apparent lack of respect in so many areas. People are elected into positions, then cheat the system and show no respect. Organizations willingly pollute the environment with no respect for the future. People litter and deface the property of others, and individuals pollute themselves with drugs and show no respect for their well-being.

Teaching the issue of respect is one that can best be found in Oriental cultures. Children are taught respect for the environment and for the members of the family. Schools can simply and elegantly unite to help children with this vital issue.

School rules need to go beyond "Don't run in the halls" and "Don't talk without raising your hand," to the issue of respect. Why don't we run down the halls? We don't run down the halls because it bothers other classrooms. Why do we need to raise our hand? Because it is respectful to the teacher to wait until he/she has completed, and it is respectful to our peers to wait our turn. Children need to go beyond the simple rules and begin to think about the reasons and actions that result from the establishment of rules.

Attempt to make the word *respect* a special word with your children. Use it when speaking with the highest regard about a situation, such as "Susan, I really respect the way you invited our new student to join you for lunch." This small act of kindness is regarded by the student and teacher as significant.

Finally, respect your students. Children deserve to be respected for their ideas, beliefs, behaviors and for their knowledge of the world as they know it. Teachers need to realize that children are in some ways more in touch with true human nature and some children understand the world better than adults. As we get older we lose the wisdom of childhood. It is important to honor and respect that important element in the children we teach.

GA1339

Manners

Good manners tell a great deal about a person. Saying "hello" and addressing a person by his name, expressing thanks, waiting your turn, using the word *please* and in general being a polite person can benefit the individual and all of society. It is important to teach children simple manners and expect that those manners be displayed in your classroom.

The best way to teach good manners is to model good manners. Use the words *thank you* and *may I* with your children whenever possible. Here are a few other suggestions.

- Ask the children to call you by your name. I have walked into primary classrooms in the springtime and the children are still calling the teacher, "teacher." When the children do call you "teacher," just look at the child and repeat your name and give them an opportunity to use your name.

- Children will walk into a room at the beginning of a day and leave at the end without ever saying "hello" or "good-bye." Greet the children in the morning with a "hello" and say "good-bye" to them at the close of the day. Use their names in the greetings and encourage them to use your name.

- If children have an opportunity to eat in your room, discuss simple etiquette such as waiting until everyone is served before you begin eating and sharing with everyone if something is made available. Table manners can also fall into this area, although what fork to use doesn't really become an issue in third grade.

- I always address my children as "ladies and gentlemen" and expect them to act in that manner. We all rise to the level of expectation.

- As the teacher, make sure you model situations where you have to wait your turn. This can take place at the water fountain or the lunch line. Show the children that you also wait your turn. Children follow the positive role model provided by the teacher.

- "Excuse me" and "I'm sorry" are important words and should be expressed by the teacher and the children. Even little situations such as bumps or a child being slighted should be followed by a word of kindness.

- Good manners express respect and give the people who use good manners the cutting edge. Having good manners is a tool for each child and is best taught through modeling by the teacher.

GA1339

Children Are Not Interested in Being Your Press Agent

Parent: "What did you do in school today?"
Child: "Nothin'."
Parent: "Well, you couldn't have done nothing. What did you learn in social studies?"
Child: "We don't have social studies."

Communication with parents is one of the most important and worthwhile tasks for teachers, students, the school and the community. You are part of a human service organization and the community needs to have a clear understanding of what you are doing and your views on education.

Newsletters are an easy vehicle for communication. The next page has some clip and copy items for your newsletter. Make sure that you check all the grammar and spelling in your letter and give a copy to the principal before the letter goes home to parents.

Calling home to parents with good news as well as bad news is essential. If teachers call only for negative reasons, eventually parents don't want to receive the calls. If you have a child with a discipline problem, in particular, it is more important to call home to report improved behavior than it is to call home to report poor behavior.

Invite parents to visit the classroom and visit with the children. Open House is the most traditional but Grandparents' Day and Community Day are also becoming popular.

Find the hidden talents of your community members. Some parents might enjoy helping with a small party or becoming involved with a cooking or craft project. Parent volunteers who work with children are a gift to many teachers who need additional help with particular children.

Finally, parents can become your advocates or your enemies. That relationship is usually determined by the teacher. Make every attempt to facilitate a positive attitude with your students, parents and the community.

GA1339

Letterheads
Clip and Copy

We Could Use Some Help

Look at What We're Doing!

Report from Our Field Trip

This Month

We Need Help Collecting Some Materials

We're Cooking

Look What's Coming Up

We've Finally Landed

85

GA1339

Stuff for Kids of Any Age

1. All children love having a chance to win. If you are looking for a motivational tool, have a raffle. Everyone likes a chance to win something.

2. Children of all ages love little rewards of stickers, candy, pencils or stamps and extra time with the teacher.

3. Children love animals. Children enjoy a class pet or a visit from animals. A few children may be unsure, but every child will show interest.

4. Children enjoy cooking. This can amount to making peanut butter and jelly sandwiches or something more detailed. Whatever the recipe, you can be assured that children will enjoy the process.

5. Children love putting on plays and telling stories. They also enjoy watching the plays and stories. If costumes are involved, the level of interest is increased.

6. Along the same lines, children love puppets. Even older children can be caught by talented use of a puppet. If you don't do puppet voices very well, have the puppet whisper into your ear.

7. Children enjoy dumb humor. They like to laugh and find many things funny. Try to incorporate humor into your classroom and teach the difference between humor, rude behavior and ridicule.

8. Children enjoy younger children. The big brother and big sister come out in children when they meet up with younger children. The best side of children will come forward when they are asked to work with a younger child.

9. Children love clerical responsibility from taking attendance, grading papers and checking in seatwork. The most prized job is taking the note to the office.

10. Children are awed by magic. Every teacher should be able to do at least one magic trick that cannot be figured out by the children. It gives you an air of mystery and raises your esteem with the children.

11. Children love a good story. If a teacher reads a good story to a group of children, that story and that teacher forever live in the life and mind of that child.

12. Children love people who love them.

13. Children love limericks and poems that are sassy and silly such as Shel Silverstein's work.

14. Children think friends are very important. Never underestimate the importance to children of having friends, being well liked and dealing with relationships.

15. Children love parties, holidays and any reason to have a little food, some games and a good time. Don't deny them the experience—everyone needs to party.

GA1339

16. Children tell the best stories about their injuries. Every child has a personal recollection of the huge splinter or the time he fell from the tree and broke his arm.

17. Children love the opportunity to touch things. They especially like to touch things that they are not normally allowed to touch such as breakable items or dangerous items such as knives and matches. Teachers can ward off the need to explore the unknown by providing safe items for children to touch that are wonderful yet harmless. Examples might be beautiful rocks and crystals or a small appliance that can be taken apart.

18. Children love bubbles and bubble wands. Even the most sophisticated child will want a turn at the bubble wand.

19. Children enjoy classroom customs. These are unwritten rules or activities that "we always do." These customs give unity, and they also give the students security in knowing what is expected.

20. Children enjoy paints. When the teacher brings out the paints, the children respond with enthusiasm and creativity.

21. Children enjoy playing at the chalkboard. The chalkboard may represent the authority of the teacher. It may be that children love writing and erasing. Whatever the reason, most children enjoy time at the board.

22. Children love to see and hear their names, anywhere and anytime.

23. Whether we like them or not, children love fads.

Sexist Roles in Your Classroom

The decades of the 60's and 70's helped bring the issue of sexist roles into focus. Today we assume that the message we send to all children is that they can be whatever they want to be. So, go ask your children. Can a boy be a nurse? Can a mommy work in a steel mill? Most children will tell you that boys can't be nurses and mommies can't work in steel mills. Children still establish sexist roles at a very young age, and those roles are difficult to break.

Talking about sexist roles needs to step outside of the social studies curriculum and the careers unit. We need to look at the daily messages we send children in subtle and yet very pervasive ways. For example, do you ask the boys to carry the garbage cans and the girls to straighten the books? Do you assume that boys like dinosaurs and that girls like Barbie dolls? Do you expect the boys to run faster and the girls to be just a bit slower? Do you expect girls to be quiet and boys to be active?

Every day, in hundreds of ways, we define ourselves. Here is a fun test to define yourself.

Are you chocolate or vanilla
      young or old
      funny or serious
      organized or messy
      loud or soft
      different or the same
      slow or fast

These definitions tell more about you just as your sex tells more about you. It should not limit you as an individual or define you as less than you can potentially become. The same goes for your children. Being a girl or a boy should be a biological fact and not a definition of his/her possibilities. Be observant and reflective of the subtle messages you send your children.

Ladies and Gentlemen

I have always referred to my children as "ladies and gentlemen" instead of boys and girls. To my way of thinking it expresses a level of expectation. Those titles reflect the best attributes of each sex that emcompass respect, politeness, gentleness and kindness.

GA1339

Please Read

Children of all ages need to be read to. As a matter of fact, people of all ages need to be read to. One of my fondest memories is of my cousin reading to me and my elderly grandmother. Grandma loved the stories, but I remember just enjoying the sound of the words. I was too young to understand, but I was fascinated by the cadence of my cousin's voice.

When we read to children, there is no outcome or expectation for student performance. Sometimes teachers may see this as a waste of time or unproductive time. It is hard to see the impact reading has on children and how it affects their own ability to read, understand story context and decode words. Teachers can read stories to children that are above their reading levels. Reading aloud gives students an opportunity to hear new vocabulary, relate to a story in an ongoing manner, see and hear a story unfold from beginning to end and most of all develop a love of the written word.

It is essential that teachers choose quality literature when reading to the class. Stories need to have lives of their own, and they need to relate to the children in your classroom.

Being a Storyteller

Storytelling is a different form of sharing literature. A storyteller usually tells his story from memory and uses his voice, hands and body to dramatize the story. This age-old art form is coming back in style, and it can be very fun for the storyteller and the audience.

The storyteller has direct eye contact with the audience and can bring them quickly into the story. Children are so taken with this type of storytelling that months later they will ask for a particular story. Each child has his own mental image of the story characters and setting. This is a wonderful strategy for use with whole language.

The storyteller needs to memorize the story and think about the character development. Fables and folktales are excellent sources for gathering stories. This art form is one that can easily be developed and a trick that can always be pulled from the hat when a little something extra is needed. Start with simple stories and make up interesting details as you go along. That's the fun. The story becomes your own.

GA1339

Indoor Recess

Indoor recess is dreaded by most teachers, rightfully so! Children need to run outside and blow off some steam during recess time. Indoor recess called because of bad weather means that children have to contain that pent up energy through lunch and into the afternoon.

The trick to a successful indoor recess is to have enough material to keep the children busy and have things that keep their interest.

Make sure to set the ground rules before recess begins and tell the children what is and is not allowed. For example, are they allowed to use the chalkboard or can they use the computer?

Children may need to be reminded that the teacher's desk is off limits and that they must respect everyone's property. Some situations work best if the children are allowed to move their desks to create a larger playing area for different games.

Some teachers have the children keep coloring books, reading material and word searches or crossword puzzles for this time. Remember that this should not turn into a work time for the children. Available activities should be relaxing and interesting to the child.

Games Made by Children

Having enough classroom games can be difficult for the teacher. It is hard to make enough games and buying them is expensive. I suggest that some classroom games be made by the students. These follow along the lines of games that are made by the teacher, but the difference is that the children are making the game parts, putting the game together, teaching each other how to play the game and taking care of the game storage and parts.

Hamburger, Fries and a Coke Game

The possibilities are endless with this game. The children color, cut and paste the game parts on tagboard. You can laminate if necessary, but a new game can also be made by next year's students. The skills could be anything that is being taught such as words that make sentences—the hamburgers are the nouns, the fries the verbs and the Cokes the adjectives. Or the hamburger could be the top number, the fries the middle and the Coke the answer. The possibilities are endless. The games can be created within the classroom and then used during free time, or a group of students can create the game and teach the remainder of the students. Children will really get excited about the learning tools when they are involved. Search through your other teaching material to find other examples for holidays and other units or themes that support the game idea.

GA1339

Hamburger, Fries and a Coke Game

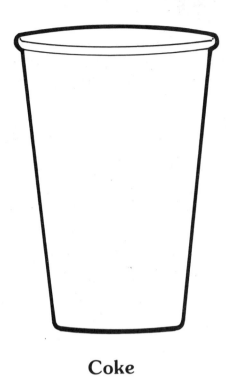

Coke

Hamburger

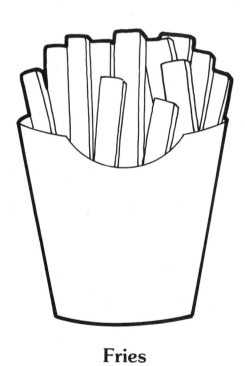

Fries

Rules

Store game parts in a fast food hamburger container.

Fads and Kids

Dick Tracy, Ninja Turtles, Batman, Barbie, Strawberry Shortcake and He-Man are only a few of the characters that have become favorites of children. These characters and other fads come to school with children every day and are a part of the American culture. A problem can arise when all the children's play and thoughts center on the fads. Teachers need to decide if they should go along with the fad or discourage it in the classroom. In other words, do you use the characters on the bulletin board but not allow them in the journal writing? How do we distinguish the need for group identity in a common interest and a counter culture of children thinking about the next cartoon show?

Here are a few guidelines for all teachers who face the American youth culture head on.

- Watch the TV shows that the children are watching and listen to the music. Decide if there is any character that could be used to reinforce a lesson or be a topic of discussion. For example, is one character always having difficulty with his peers, or is one character the bully?
- If the fad is an object such as little cars, baseball cards, figures, dolls or balls, then the presence of these objects in the classroom may become a problem. Children will carry them back and forth to school and sometimes the toy is stolen or misplaced. Other times the children want to play with them during recess. General rules concerning toys need to be established from the beginning of the year.
- Sometimes fads and action play become overextended for some young children. They become super heroes out on the playground and bash their playmates in the excitement of the play. The element of fantasy needs to be discussed with young children.
- These characters can motivate children and increase their interest in some subjects, but they can also act as distractors. Children may replay their cartoons in their thoughts rather than the lesson.
- School is a place where new, exciting characters can be introduced to children through their literature and the teacher's read-alouds. These should also be included in the classroom culture.

GA1339

What's Taught Is Not Always What's Caught

A Word from the Wise

Dr. Chuck Richards
Goshen Community Schools
Assistant Superintendent
Indiana

You don't realize how literal young children take what you tell them. As part of my first teaching assignment, I taught physical education to kindergarten children. The kindergarten teacher was thrilled to have someone teach this class and told her children all week about getting to go to "gym." When gym day arrived I know that I introduced myself, but as the children left the gym, they waved good-bye and said, "Bye, Jim, see you next week."

Children aren't the only ones who get mixed messages as this next story will illustrate. As new teachers we are anxious to get off to a great start and do everything correctly. But even adults get mixed messages.

A Word from the Wise

Ruth Bond
Avon, Connecticut

I entered the teaching profession after having my children. I got my first job in a Cleveland Catholic school, and I was thrilled. The first week of school the principal, a nun, called over the public address system into my room, "Ruth, would you send your records to the office."

I loaded the arms of two children and moments later Sister was standing at my door laughing to the point of tears. Every feeling crossed over me at that moment as she said, "Ruth, I want your students' records, not your record albums."

Everyone is allowed to make some mistakes. Relax and go with the flow!

GA1339

Feeling Successful at Every Level

I once had a conversation with a friend of mine who teaches physics. He explained to me that one of his teaching goals was to give every student a sense of success despite his grade in the class. He said that some students will be able to leave his class and teach physics to other students, some will leave with a fair understanding and an ability to apply the principles and others will leave with the minimum understanding. Each of these students should leave that classroom feeling proud of what he did learn and what he was able to achieve.

All too often we focus on the negative, and we fail to acknowledge the positive components to our learning and of our abilities. Each of us has a different capacity for learning different subjects, and we should help children feel comfortable within their ability range.

Working at Your Own Pace

Have you ever eaten with a slow eater? Do we rush them along to the next part of the meal and tell them to put down that fork, it's time to stop? Of course we don't behave in this manner, and yet this is exactly what we do to children who are slow workers. Some children take more time to complete their work than others. They may twist and turn and look at the ceiling while they think and ponder the answers.

As teachers we may say things like "move along, times up, cleanup time" or "you're in for recess." Some children are slowpokes out of laziness, but some children are slow to process. It is important, as the teacher, that you can identify one from the other and give appropriate time to those who need it.

GA1339

Pull-Out Programs

With the new demands for accountability and the demand for attention to the special needs of children, teachers have found themselves in a situation where children come and go from the classroom at an alarming pace. Here are samples of some of the programs that may be pull-outs (the child leaves the classroom to work with another person) in your building.

Music instructional lessons
Speech therapy
Gifted and talented programs
Remedial reading
Student council
Computer or media instruction

Safety patrol
Learning disabled
Chapter I
Math tutor
Classroom helper
Physically, visually or aurally impaired

Some of these may fit your situation and others may not pertain. If a child leaves your classroom, is the child responsible for the work you covered in his absence? What about tests and evaluation? Will the child know the material if he missed the lesson? Does the teacher have the time to reteach on a daily basis? Those are just a few questions that come up when children leave the room.

The professionals who work with our children deserve to have our cooperation and respect. They are interested in the child's progress and are generally working in small groups with the children. Talk to the specialist about the child and work together to get material covered.

Help your children keep up with what they missed by keeping the assignments on the chalkboard. As we attempt to teach independent study skills, it is always helpful to have the child take some ownership for finding out what needs to be done.

Assign children buddies that help keep each other informed as to what is happening and what needs to be completed. Check your school policy on work that is missed due to a pull-out program. Is the child responsible for the knowledge and not the work? Make sure you know how to address parents' concerns.

Is It Time?

Young children have a difficult time knowing where they are supposed to go and when they are supposed to leave. The "clock watcher" can help the children keep the time and remind them of their assigned pull-out programs. Once the schedule is established, these can be laminated and taped to the inside of the desk for a reminder to the child.

GA1339

Speech	Reading	Math $\frac{\begin{array}{r}2\\+5\end{array}}{7}$	Computer	Safety	Chapter I	Teacher

Place:

Teacher's Name:

Room:

Notes:

Place:

Teacher's Name:

Room:

Notes:

Place:

Teacher's Name:

Room:

Notes:

Put a picture in the place for nonreaders.

GA1339

Working with High-Risk Students

High-risk students can be classified into that category for a variety of reasons. They may have poor organizational skills and are unable to complete their work. They may have been premature babies born with a low birth weight and are having difficulty because they are still developmentally delayed. A child with very poor social skills may be considered high risk, or a child with a very short attention span may suffer school difficulties. The variety of problems that children can bring to school are endless. The issue for the teacher is to identify the children with problems and attempt to discover what can be done to help them.

There is one solution that works for every child, no matter what kind of delay or problem may exist. The solution that works with every child is building positive self-esteem. It is a solution that can never fail to improve the situation. Every individual needs to feel he is special and has abilities that make him stand apart from the crowd. Having a positive self-esteem is one of the most powerful forces in any individual's life. Here are some suggestions for children who are high risk in your classroom.

- Find their talents. If necessary, make one up such as best brush cleaner or best gardener.

- Have the high-risk child tutor a much younger child who is having difficulty.

- Provide private praise and make sure it is sincere.

- Set the child up for success. Provide situations that will only lead one way—up.

- Help the child become a class expert on some portion of the class activities or a particular subject area.

- Spend time listening to the high-risk child and attempt to understand the child's feelings.

These guidelines actually fit for all children but are absolutely necessary for high-risk students. They have issues and difficulties that bother them daily. These problems will be buried and will build a negative self-image that tells them they are not capable and stupid. Children can overcome what they think they can overcome. Giving children a belief in themselves and their abilities is one of education's most important goals.

GA1339

Working with Talented Students

Some children have wonderful art skills. I once taught a kindergarten student who tested a fourth grade level and higher in every subject area. Some children come to school with outstanding athletic skills, and others are very social and wonderful with all ages of people. Each of us has our own talent and ability that should be recognized and acknowledged.

Some children come to school with extraordinary abilities. It may be difficult to find enough to satisfy the quest for knowledge, or the child may excel in the things he/she likes and fail the disliked subjects. The other classmates may resent the child because he or she may never seem to fail or even stumble. Sometimes talented students just end up with a larger volume of work to complete.

Make sure that the reading material is at the child's level. That may mean they are working alone, but that child needs to have experiences reading within the comfort zone of his/her ability. Work that is too easy quickly becomes boring and meaningless, and work that is too difficult can frustrate.

Find the talents of each child within your classroom and match the children into pairs to work on a project that reflects each of their talents. The academically talented child may work with the artistically talented child. Teachers need to reinforce to the children that success in school does not equal success in the world. Being a valedictorian does not ensure success in life. Hard work, understanding of people and a willingness to be the best you can be is just as likely to bring about success for any individual.

Rather than look for new content areas to explore with the talented child, look deeper into the presented subject material. Simple questions can raise the level for a talented child when the teacher asks a question that demands comparison or synthesis of a concept.

Don't give talented students more work, give them a higher quality of work that reflects their abilities and interests. Highly successful students may have difficulty dealing with their areas of need. Some talented students may be socially shy or poor in their gross motor skills. The teacher should attempt to round the students and help them to reach their full potential in all areas.

Finally, don't favor the talented children. It is easy to give them added attention if they are interested and engaged in the learning process. Attempt to find ways that they can share that enthusiasm and get other students thinking and learning.

A Word from the Wise

Rita Marie Hemmert
Washoe County School District
Kindergarten Teacher
Reno Sparks, Nevada

Rita reminds teachers to:

- Be a child advocate. Work with the system to help a child get the help or services he needs. Be persistent, firm and fight for the child if necessary.

- Be honest with parents. Don't gloss over a problem. Be direct and caring. You will gain the parents' respect and their confidence.

- Have parent helpers in your room. They are your best advocates. Parent helpers see what happens and will support the teacher within the community.

- Wear a smile and laugh with your children.

- Always be open to new ideas, techniques, teaching strategies and philosophies. Listen, learn and then decide how or if it fits into your style of teaching.

Notable Quote

Don't be afraid to try something new, I thought carrots were terrible until I tasted sauerkraut.

Hank Ketcham
"Dennis the Menace"

GA1339

Humor

Humor is an important element in any classroom. It is a funny place where funny things happen. Teachers need to create an atmosphere where children feel free to laugh and giggle. It is hard to imagine a group of children who are without humor, sitting at their desks, quiet and lifeless.

The caution with humor is to be sensitive to the fact that no individual should be the brunt of the joke. The teacher should be cautious to watch the children in groups to make sure one child is not being ridiculed by the others.

Children love to see the teacher foul up. Mistakes on the chalkboard that the teacher keeps insisting are correct and the children intervening to correct the teacher are funny and great teaching tools. Funny limericks, poems and stories are popular with children. They respond well to familiar situations and objects that are misplaced or out of their environment such as "What is wrong with this picture?" or footprints on the ceiling of the room that lead to a learning center.

A Word from the Wise

Linda Johnson
Retired Special Education Source Teacher
Anchorage, Alaska

One day, during my first year of teaching thirty years ago, I developed a huge hole in the knee of my nylon. When standing up, in my straight, below-the-knee skirt, no one could see it, but when I sat down guess what! One of my students started giggling—then a couple more—and soon we all had the giggles. I think I realized that day the importance of sharing laughter with my kids, and perhaps even more important, the kids saw me laughing at myself.

Making Mistakes

Children should make mistakes—lots of mistakes—every day, and they should be taught that one of the best ways to learn is through their mistakes. These mistakes should be academic mistakes and behavioral mistakes. Testing the boundaries and making mistakes is one of the inherent privileges of being a child.

Academic Mistakes

Making mistakes and correcting those mistakes need to be an integral part of every classroom experience. Mistakes are not necessarily the wrong answer but the pathway to the right answer or answers.

An analogy might be learning to ride a bicycle. As a child learns to ride, he falls off the bike many times. The bike tips, turns, he falls and scrapes his knees and hands. Each try is one step closer to the day that child can ride the bike alone. The mistakes teach the child about the dynamics of the bike, and he learns how to correct his balance and ride the bike.

When a child makes a mistake and the teacher addresses the mistake, that is the teachable moment. It is at that moment children and teacher work together to balance the bike. If work sheets are given to children and they make mistakes, then an opportunity should be provided to correct those mistakes. When a child corrects his mistake, he may realize what he did wrong and learn from that.

Behavior Mistakes

Children also need to make mistakes in their behavior. Every baby pinched, bit, screamed, took toys from playmates, cried for no reason and fought. Some children take longer than others to realize that as inappropriate behavior and most children will stop the biting by the time they graduate from high school.

When children get to school they have another set of mistakes that they learn to control, and for some children it takes longer to learn control than others. These behaviors may be excessive talking, teasing, fighting, uncontrolled anger or aggression, refusal to work or stealing. Learning how to control your feelings and making responsible decisions is a lesson that we spend a lifetime learning. School is one of the primary environments where these lessons will be learned.

GA1339

Home Visits

The opportunity to visit the homes of the children you teach is one of the most treasured acts remembered by parents, students and teachers. Making the commitment to visit every child's home is a commitment of time, energy, generosity and openness to the variety of lifestyles and values of your students.

A home visit can be a fun visit where the children plan a special activity for the teacher. Or the visit can be more formal and the teacher, parent and child can talk about the child and his/her progress.

Make sure that during the visit you spend some time with the child and center your attention on the things the child wants to share. Parents will tend to pull the teacher into conversation, but make sure that the child has an ample amount of your undivided attention.

Be sensitive to the variety of situations you will be viewing in the home. This is a great experience for new teachers since it gives valuable insight into various student and family situations. Be an observer and a participant during the visit, but don't be a judge. Don't judge what you will see as good or bad, positive or negative or any other ways, for it is our job as teachers to teach all children equally and with compassion and love.

Finally, set the time limit on the visit before your arrival so that families are not preparing meals unnecessarily or missing appointments. Be gracious in every situation and make sure to send a thank-you note for the kind hospitality. Being welcomed into a home is a privilege and in every situation should be seen as a special honor.

Approval

Children love approval. Actually everyone loves approval. When someone gives you approval, it raises your self-esteem and says you are important and special. As humans, we shouldn't rely on others to help us improve our self-esteem, but for better or worse it exists as a character trait of most individuals.

Almost every veteran teacher I have ever met has a box that contains little notes and scraps of paper that say something that is nice about their teaching. Notes written by parents or a little note pad from the principal about a bulletin board makes people feel recognized and that they are successful. Those same basic human needs exist in every child.

Approval should be personal if at all possible. A child could receive a little note that says, "I like the way you are trying during recess," or "Good job on that spelling test last week; you are getting better and better at spelling." I have found one of the most powerful forms of approval is a private conversation with the child. Pulling him aside and telling him that he is doing a terrific job in a particular area is very motivating to a child.

Approval should be given to everyone at some time or another. Look for the most difficult children to do something well and then jump on the chance to praise the positive. Don't overdo the praise; keep it sincere and honest.

Don't forget to give approval to other people in your building. Notes to fellow teachers about their school projects or notes to the principal that express appreciation or a job well done will be positively received.

Approval is not stamps or stickers on papers. Approval is a personal moment when you say to the other individual, "You have done well, and it is noticed and appreciated."

GA1339

Completion = Celebration

I sat in my graduate class and watched the students after finishing the midterm exam. When they completed the exam, they stretched and looked around the room. Many of them began to make noise as they gathered up their belongings and headed out to the hallway where they could talk with other students. These are the same students who seldom linger after class on a regular basis. I began to watch all sorts of groups, and I found that whenever a task was completed it called for a small celebration.

We know that when we do work around our homes we may treat ourselves to something small like a drink of iced tea or a minute to read the paper after a job is completed. Children in the classroom do the very same thing, and they usually celebrate by talking. When a child completes a paper, a set of problems or a reading assignment, he looks for a little celebration. It might come in the form of a chat with a neighbor, a trip to the pencil sharpener or a visit to the bathroom. Most children and adults need to take a break after the completion of a task.

The problem for the teacher is that many of the children may begin to talk to others who have not completed their work. They may disturb the environment and distract the quiet children. The first trick to solving this problem is acknowledging that a mini celebration after a task is completed is a reality. The second is to find some appropriate mini celebration solutions.

Viewfinders

Do you remember the wonderful old viewfinders? The array of pictures on disks are endless. Why not place a viewfinder next to the basket for completed work and have the pictures relate to something being studied. After the work is turned in, the child gets to make a once-around with the viewfinder to read the captions and look at the pictures.

Sand Escape

The marketplaces are filled with executive toys that are supposed to relieve stress. Little containers that make rows of oil-filled droplets, sand that looks like mountains and deserts and key chains that carry little water games are just a few. These can also be placed on the "take a break" table for those children who have completed their work.

Mini celebrations will take place whether we give our permission or not. We might as well make these celebrations work to our advantage and to the children's advantage.

GA1339

Everyone Is a Winner

Have you ever played musical chairs with a group of four-year-olds? Well don't! This is the game where you are always playing with one chair too few and every round of play produces a loser. Children cry and try to squeeze on the chair with another child. Some children leave the game angry and others just feel hurt.

Don't set up situations in your classroom with unnecessary competition that creates sure losers. Some teachers only put up the excellent papers creating the winner/loser syndrome. Other teachers post grades or read the grades out loud so that the winners and losers are quickly identified. Contrary to popular belief, this does nothing for motivation toward excellence. Most children will run from their failures, as will most adults. How many of us as adults gravitate to activities that we have found unsuccessful? By the time we're adults, most of us come right out and say, "I don't sew" or "I'm not good at plumbing." We could learn, but these are not the areas where we have experienced past success.

Create a classroom filled with winners. This is almost impossible, but get as close to the ideal as possible and you will have a classroom that is truly full of winners.

Let Students Compete Against Themselves

One surefire technique is to let the children work against themselves rather than each other. Keep journals so the children can witness their growth. Help them keep their grades on spelling tests and other work.

Student of the Day

At the end of every day the teacher can acknowledge one or more students who were students of the day. An act of kindness, improved behavior, cooperative learner or any other observed behavior can be used by the teacher to choose the designated student. This gives every child a chance to be a winner, and it recognizes behavior that doesn't require academic talent.

Pride Wall

The pride wall is a place where any student can place work that he is proud of doing. Everyone must respect the wall and the work placed on the wall. This gives children a chance to say, "I worked hard on this." It can also give the teacher an opportunity to view the child's perception of his best work.

GA1339

Affective Elements That Make a Classroom a Safe and Happy Place

Each person hopefully has some place where he can feel safe and secure. For some of us it may specifically be our living room or our bed. Others may feel safe in the company of their parents or family while some young children transfer their safety zone to a blanket or a pillow. In your safe place you can relax, let down and be yourself. You are a part of the environment in the safe place and things are familiar.

These are the kinds of feelings we would like to have within the classroom walls. A room where children can feel safe and are among familiar people and objects is something that is developed over time. Creating this type of safe harbor is a challenge among cold floors, hard desks, books and papers.

Here are some ideas for building a safe environment for your classroom children.

- Let the children take ownership over portions of the room, bulletin board, etc.
- Have safe places where the children can rest quietly or read to themselves. Try to create one or two comfortable spots.
- Smile at your children and get them to smile back.
- Build trust through demonstrating trust—trust the children, and let them earn trust through added responsibility.
- Children need to feel safe from ridicule brought on by their peers.
- They need to feel safe to give a wrong answer. Teacher and students have to send a message of caring for each other.
- Every child needs his own personal space. Should children be allowed to do their own "interior desk decorating"? Teachers need to have control of a clean environment but also respect the child's personal space.
- Don't be afraid to break from routine and do something as a whole group. Create the family feeling.
- Implement the children's suggestions whenever possible. Make them the owners of their environment.

You and the Structure of Schools

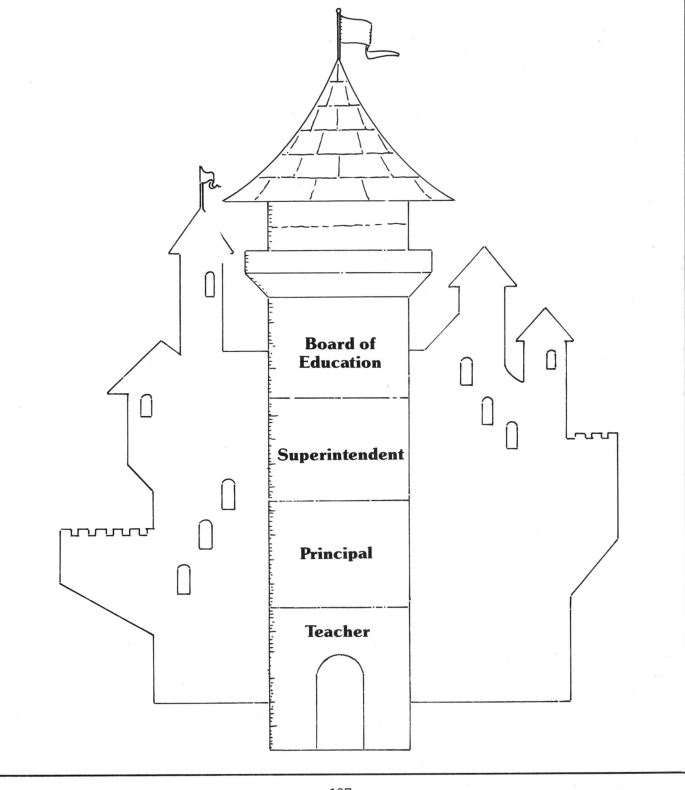

GA1339

The secret of happiness is not in doing what one likes, but in liking what one does.

James M. Barrie

The School Culture

Do you remember going to a favorite aunt's house or to Grandma's as a child? The house also smelled a certain way, and there was always a familiar look about the environment. Grandma always had a "certain way" of doing the cooking or cleaning. Certain activities needed to be taken care of on particular days and times of the year. Life was a system that had an approach that was safe and predictable.

Schools establish their own cultures with certain predictable activities and establish routines. These cultures can be found in the overall school system and within each individual building.

As a new teacher you may have many exciting ideas that will be met with the statement "We don't do that here." That resistance may be a reflection of the school culture. Individual teachers and the administration may have certain "unseen rules" that are totally hidden from the outsider's sight. It is important to learn about the culture of your environment before trying some new ideas.

Your school culture may be reflective of the community's culture. The community may be very conservative and have a social culture that is closed to anything different. If you show up for school in something trendy but very different, that culture may be offended.

In some cultures people hug and in others people don't. In some cultures people play jokes and in others they wouldn't consider playing jokes. A new teacher is being watched as to how he/she fits into the culture.

The school culture can transfer down to rules about absent children, running off dittos, sending notes to parents or attending after-school meetings. Make sure to investigate your school culture. Study the procedures, expectations and unseen rules.

GA1339

Serving on School Committees

Serving on a school committee is one of the best ways new teachers can network with other staff and have opportunities for professional growth. The committees may range from social committees to writing curriculum. In either case here are a few points for reference.

- Keep to your commitments. If you volunteer to serve on a committee, make sure you work to honor that commitment. Do the necessary work in preparation for each meeting and come prepared to work.
- Be part of the collaborative process. Most committees involve numbers of people with a variety of different perspectives. Be a contributor, but don't take over or expect your views to be the final say. In these situations compromise must prevail even if it doesn't seem to match your philosophy.
- People are bound to criticize. After you have volunteered your time for a committee and put in the extra hours, you may take great pride in the work that was completed. It is just about that time someone will wander up and give the project a swift kick in the pants. Don't give up and say, "Never again." Don't let the negative lead.
- You will have a much better understanding of the curriculum after serving on a committee that is involved in curriculum development. This process is a valuable growth experience and will help to establish you with other teachers in your district.
- School committees also give you an opportunity to let your views be shared. Because of your recent college experiences, as a new teacher you may have a fresher and newer approach than the veteran teachers.

GA1339

Unions:
The American Federation of Teachers(AFT)
The National Education Association (NEA)

As a new teacher you may be approached to join a teachers' union. The two largest unions in the United States are the AFT and the NEA. Each state has its own affiliate which changes the initial letter to OEA in my case, which stands for the Ohio Education Association.

If you join the union, your dues may be deducted from your pay. In most cases, joining the union will also provide you with some additional benefits in insurance and travel opportunities to name two. The real question is what does the union do for teachers?

The biggest responsibility of the union is collective bargaining. This means that union representatives bargain for salary and benefits with the school board of education and administrative team. The premise is that as a large unified body, teachers' needs will be heard.

Unions also deal with teacher grievances. A grievance usually is some sort of difference between the contract and the district or personnel expectation. The grievance may involve a policy or an innerpersonal problem. The union acts as a buffer for the teacher and mediates the problem.

If a teacher gets sued by a parent, the union will usually provide legal representation for the teacher. If your union is unified, you will be required to not only join the local but also the state and national affiliates of the union.

Joining a union occasionally may mean that the teachers will go on strike. This is always a lose-lose situation for teachers, administrators, community and children, but it is also part of the workings of a union. If your union does go out on strike, my personal advice is to join the strike. The teachers who cross the picket lines may have a difficult time with members of the staff for many months and even years after the strike. Remember that the union's strength is in the unity of the collective group.

The negative aspect of unions is that in some cases they overprotect employees. After a teacher has been tenured, it is difficult to have a teacher fired. Many very unsuccessful individuals earn large sums of money in a profession they should have been forced from decades ago. This type of teacher hurts the profession and would never survive in another competitive job. On the other hand, if someone decides he doesn't like your "style," he cannot fire you without due process and review.

Unions are an unusual part of the teaching profession. Make sure that as a professional, you exceed the contract obligations and go to the limit for your children.

GA1339

Understanding Your School Administration

School Board

In most cities the school board members are elected by the voters. The school board is a symbol of laymen control over the school administration, teachers and personnel. In theory, the school board should demonstrate community leadership and leave the management skills to the hired administrative staff. In reality school boards often become involved with school administrative issues.

Superintendent

The superintendent's role is to act as educational leader to the community. This individual should hold the values of the community and share its common mission. The superintendent answers directly to the school board and is held responsible on most issues.

Curriculum Coordinator

The individual in this position is responsible for curriculum development, curriculum implementation and possibly curriculum evaluation. This individual is the person who should be updated on new strategies through conferences and workshops. The curriculum coordinator may also be responsible for staff inservice.

Director of Personnel

The personnel director deals with issues that range from union interaction to interviewing and hiring teachers and staff. The personnel director may also be involved with community services and public relations.

Business Manager

The business manager directs the flow of workers through the system. In most communities the school is the largest "business." Schools hire the most personnel, have transportation issues, grounds keeping and maintenance concerns. Keeping the schools open and running is a very important job.

GA1339

Principals

The role of principal originated as head teacher. The head teacher was the "master teacher" in the building and the one individual who demonstrated the most mastery over the art of teaching. Ideally, the principal should remain as the educational leader for his/her building. Unfortunately, principals often get caught in the administrative paper chase and don't have the time they would like to have for sharing teaching ideas and philosophy. The principal has the responsibility to see that the curriculum is being administered and that the children are in a safe and healthy environment.

Teachers

Teachers are the "worker bees." The teacher is responsible for the implementation of all the hopes, dreams and wishes of all the above people. Sometimes the desires of the administration don't match your expectations for your job. Carefully study the materials provided by the school administration to determine your role within the school.

What to Do If You Have a Conflict

There is an unwritten rule that in the school community you must follow the chain of command if you have a complaint. This is a very important rule. Even if your best friend is the president of the board of education, go to your principal FIRST with your concern. If your principal decides not to act, then you have the right to move up the ladder, but be sure not to miss a rung. There is no doubt that this is the long, slow road to change, but it is a fact of life in almost all school districts. The exception to this rule is in the case of child abuse. As the teacher you are responsible for reporting the incident and should make sure that the lines of communication are completely open.

Principal

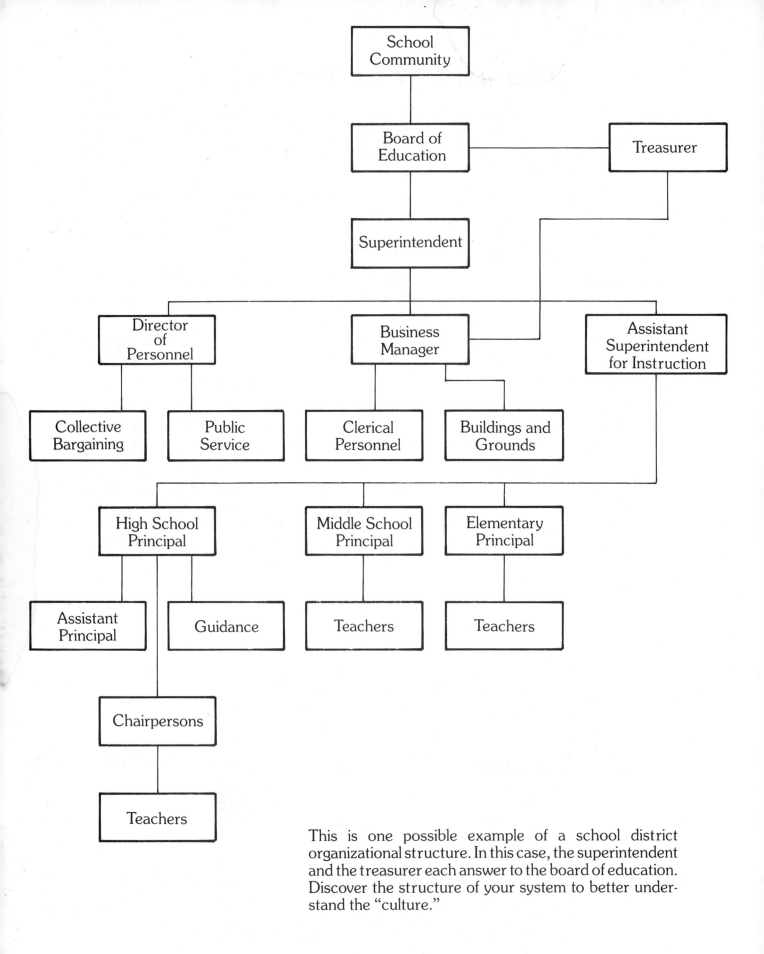

This is one possible example of a school district organizational structure. In this case, the superintendent and the treasurer each answer to the board of education. Discover the structure of your system to better understand the "culture."

114

You and Your Principal

The principal job was originally the role of master teacher. That person was the designated "expert" who could be called upon for consultations and advice. Today's principals frequently get to enjoy the role of instructional leader since most of them focus their time on administrative work.

Today's schools are a business. Schools have budgets, records, clients and building maintenance. These are just a few of the areas principals need to address. They must supervise the staff of classified and certified personnel and maintain a relationship with the parents and the community.

Your principal probably puts in hours after the school day at school events and doing the extensive paperwork required of most schools. If your district is small, then the principal may also be given additional assignments.

As a teacher you should try to understand the job of your principal. It is easy to criticize the principal until you understand that he/she must be available to irate parents, angry school boards and children who fall off playground equipment on a constant basis.

Try not to burden your principal with unnecessary concerns but do include them in all your important decisions. Make sure to share any correspondence that is sent home. Principals should be informed so if they are questioned they will be ready with a response.

Principals need praise and a pat on the back, too. Tell them when they are doing a good job. Principals also need to know what is confusing or undefined. If you are unsure about policies such as whether children may call home to get a lunch, then ask for specific instructions. Often when you begin a new job, the principal has established an unwritten set of "rules" that you must break one by one in order to discover the unwritten policy. Don't be afraid to speak up and say, "I don't know how to handle . . . ."

GA1339

Principal Visitation

Invite your principal into your room as frequently as possible. Have you ever had a special guest over for dinner? Everyone is on edge and if you have children, you have warned them many times to BEHAVE. The meal is a special feast, and the house is clean and bright.

Then there is the family dinner. Nothing special and nobody acting on his best manners. Everyone is talking and sharing at the same moment. Dishes may be left in the sink until later.

When you invite the principal into the room, it should be like the family dinner and not like a special guest. The principal should be part of your classroom family and treated as one of the group. Work toward building the relationship with the principal, the children and yourself.

GA1339

You and Your School Janitor

Be nice to this person. He/She supplies the "green stuff." Actually, janitors do a great deal more than clean up after sick children. They are responsible for the smooth running of your building facility. They do jobs such as patch roofs, clean floors, fix desks, manage the heating system, fix untold numbers of broken windows and secure the building. In many cases the principal and the janitor will be called in the middle of the night if an alarm goes off and the building is being vandalized.

Your janitor also has a relationship with the children in the building. This one individual is often the "constant." The principal and teachers may change, but your building may still have the same janitor. Children enjoy seeing the janitor, and many janitors become actively involved with the children.

The janitor also does work on the grounds around the building. This may involve acres of land and grass. The summer months provide time for painting rooms, repaving walkways and repairing plumbing. It is a very important job and one that is never recognized until something goes wrong.

Don't forget to include your janitor in an activity; invite him/her in for a snack or include him/her on a field trip. Praise his/her hard work and tell him/her that the building is "looking good" once in a while.

GA1339

You and Your Building Specialists

Your building may have a number of teachers who are involved with your classroom students such as Chapter I teachers, gifted teachers, physical education teachers, librarians, speech teachers, guidance counselors or art teachers. These individuals will have a continuing impact on your children. It is important to keep up the communication and share your knowledge of the child and areas of concern.

These specialists can be invaluable to the goals of the teacher concerning specific children. They can reinforce your objectives for anything from organizational skills for a particular student to developing better fine motor skills. Having another teacher work with the children on the same area can be very supportive and productive for children.

Teachers should also tap into the expertise of these individuals. If you need ideas for some outdoor games, talk to the gym teacher and if you are unsure how to work with a child who has poor speech habits, talk to the speech teacher. These teachers enjoy the opportunity to share their knowledge, and I have never found one that wasn't willing to give some free advice.

Finally, remember that these folks may see every child in your school. They have to plan and meet the needs of children who have difficult problems and in many cases are suffering from school failure. Share your knowledge of children and support their requests for assistance whenever possible. Their participation in the school makes it a better place for everyone.

GA1339

You and Your Room Mothers

Room mothers are a time-honored tradition in schools. At one time, room mothers were one of the few ways parents could become involved with their children's school. Today most schools have extensive school volunteer parent programs.

Room mothers are usually involved with holiday parties and projects such as cooking or field trips. Every school handles the situation of room mothers differently, but it is important to remember a few tips.

- If room mothers come in for parties, do not leave them totally in charge of the class. They do not know the children and may not be able to handle the discipline during this high excitement activity.
- Let room mothers know what you like and don't like. If you want to steer clear of gooey cupcakes and ice cream, let them know. If you want games and prizes for everyone, share that information.
- Help parents anticipate problems. The parents may not realize that some activities may cause too much of a disturbance or that some children will be upset if the game knocks players out by elimination such as musical chairs. Different ages of children can handle different types of activities, and parents need to be educated as to what is appropriate.
- If parents come in to help with an activity, remind them that they are there to supervise the activity and not DO the activity. I will never forget the kindergarten parents who, to my chagrin, cut every apple for the applesauce instead of letting the children work with the table knives.
- Finally, be sure to remember your room mothers at Christmas and the end of the year. Nice notes and stationery or a small candle and card will be appreciated. These parents give the extra all of us require to do these extras with our children.

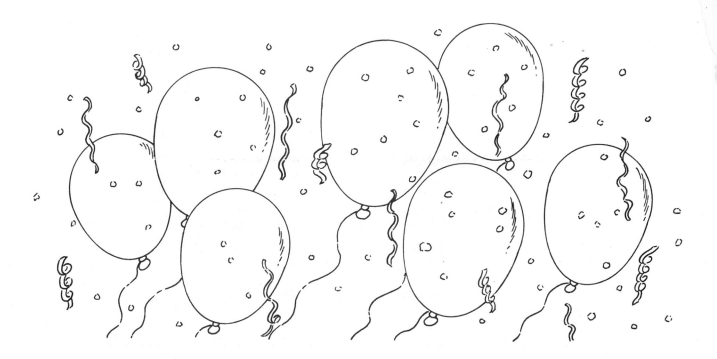

GA1339

You and Your School Secretary

The truth must be told. The school secretary runs your school. He/She knows where everything is and how to get his/her hands on all sorts of materials. He/She knows the parents and the children. The school secretary is generally the first person to meet a visitor to the school and welcomes the new families. The school secretary understands the culture of your school better than anyone.

Your school secretary may be responsible for putting bandages on playground cuts, calling parents for sick children and acting as second in command when the principal is not in the building.

Being a school secretary is an amazing job. These wonderful people have the kind of job that never gets done. The interruptions are endless, and the amount of work is staggering.

I have always tried to keep my expectations for personal service from the school secretary to a minimum. Requests for typed letters, help with special projects and programs should be as limited as possible. If each teacher were to make special requests, you can imagine the volume of work the secretary would have to complete.

Remember to notify the school secretary of changes that affect the record keeping. Get your attendance to the office on time in the morning, and notify the secretary of children who have moved. Share notes that require specific attention to the children such as medicine, illness or late pickup with the secretary. The secretary needs to be informed of all the little details. If a child gets on the wrong bus, the secretary will get the call, and if a parent has a complaint, the secretary will likely hear about it first.

Finally, remember these unsung heroes with a treat for the holidays; invite them into your room when you have a special event and listen to their concerns. In many cases the school secretary is the foundation of the building.

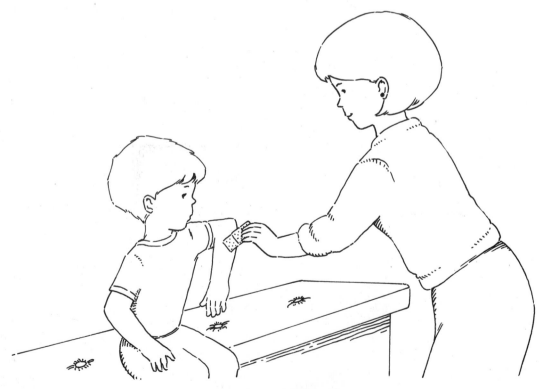

You and the School Cleaning Staff

The school cleaning staff has the responsibility to clean up the building and get it ready for the next day of school. Some buildings have a staff of two or three for a building with thirty or more classrooms. During the day hundreds of children have marched through those halls and rooms leaving trails of paper, mud and pencil shavings.

The children and teacher should be responsible for the major cleanup in a classroom. Together they should monitor the paper and general mess that accumulates. Children should put up their chairs at the end of the day to make the job easier for the cleaning staff. Teachers should make sure the room is in order before leaving.

I have seen some teachers who think the cleaning staff should be responsible for cleaning up paint and brushes left from the day's activities, food left out from lunch, toys and games left on the floor. These are not the responsibility of the cleaning staff. The room should be in order at the end of the day, and the cleaning staff should be able to come in and clean sinks, bathrooms, floors and do general housecleaning.

Make sure to dust the room and keep your own desk clean. Your environment needs to have a clean look, and a room with many children needs maintenance. Don't leave that job to the cleaning staff. Pitch in with the children and get the job done.

GA1339

In Conclusion

There is no other job like teaching. Teachers are given nine months to influence and teach a group of individuals—a group of people with their own set of needs, strengths and personalities. The job has no clear beginning and no set end. Some lessons have to do with life and not with academics.

The job of teaching is a noble and rewarding profession even on the toughest of days. Imagine a job description that asks someone to:

ignite imaginations
soothe emotions
create magic
encourage thinking
inspire humor
teach organization
create an environment
communicate with parents

provide artistic experiences
teach independence
maintain total order
teach social skills
provide social organization
keep updated on new strategies
teach the curriculum
be a role model

It's a big job but one that is in the very capable hands of teachers. Teachers influence each child's journey and are the guides that lead all children into the future.

GA1339